LEARNING ABOUT GOD... FROM A TO Z

by MARY E. ERICKSON

Sonlight Curriculum Ltd.

ISBN 1-887840-05-2

Cover illustration by Robert Gunn
Inside drawings by Ron Wheeler

Unless otherwise noted, Scripture quotations in this publication are from the *Holy Bible: New International Version* (NIV). Copyright © 1973, 1978, 1984, International Bible Society. Used by permission of Zondervan Bible Publishers. Other versions used include: *The Living Bible* (TLB), © 1971 owned by assignment by Illinois Regional Bank N.A. (as trustee), used by permission of Tyndale House Publishers, Inc., Wheaton, IL 60189; and the *King James Version* (KJV).

Printed in the United States of America

First printing by NavPress, a ministry of the Navigators—1989.
First Sonlight Curriculum Printing, 1992.
Current edition printed by Sonlight Curriculum, Ltd., 1996.
Reprinted by arrangement with the author.

For a catalog of Sonlight Curriculum materials for the home school, send $2 to

Sonlight Curriculum, Ltd.
8042 South Grant Way
Littleton, CO 80122
USA

CONTENTS

To Wally—
my husband and best friend—
for his love and confidence,
his patience and prayers,
his input and support.

Mary Erickson has been enthusiastically involved with children and teenagers all her adult life. As a pastor's wife for fifteen years, she invested her time in youth, teaching Sunday school classes and directing children's churches and choirs, daily vacation Bible schools, and summer camps. She also spent four years teaching in Seoul, South Korea. She occasionally travels with her husband, the President of Compassion International, to other countries where over 100,000 children are learning about Jesus while they study reading, writing, and arithmetic.

As a parent, Mary is the mother of three and grandmother of four. As a teacher for eleven years, she taught in elementary school, junior high, and high school. As an author, she specializes in writing for children. She has written *Adventure at Hidden Haven Ranch* for eight- to twelve-year-olds, *Jesus the Wonder-Worker* series for eight- to ten-year-olds, and *Six Busy Days* for four- to seven-year-olds.

INTRODUCTION

• • • How to Use This Activity Book • • •
(for parents and teachers)

PURPOSE

"An unknown God can neither be trusted, served, nor worshiped," wrote Dr. Earl D. Radmacher, a seminary professor.

A.W. Tozer stated in his book, *The Knowledge of the Holy*: "A right conception of God is basic not only to systematic theology, but to practical Christian living as well. It is to worship what the foundation is to the temple."

The paramount purpose of this book is to help families and students grow in their understanding of God. As you begin to learn more of God, you will enjoy a fuller, richer life.

Together your family or students will explore the Bible and learn about the attributes of God. What is an attribute? It is a distinguishing quality that reveals a person's character.

BOOK ORGANIZATION

This book has twenty-six chapters, one for each letter of the alphabet which stands for one attribute of God. It can be used in many contexts: the family, Christian schools, home schools, and Sunday schools. Throughout the book, we will be speaking in terms of the family context.

Each chapter includes Scriptures, activities, discussions, an application, a challenge, and a prayer that relate to the attribute.

There are no rules to bind you. The amount covered at each session will depend upon available time and the age, ability, and attention span of the children. You may want to divide the longer chapters into two sessions, doing the plays or memorization projects later.

There is no best way to proceed. You may work systematically through the book or design your own program. Some chapters relate well to special holidays (e.g., B, Thanksgiving; L, Christmas).

SUPPLIES NEEDED
Bibles

This project uses Scriptures from three versions of the Bible: the *New International Version* (NIV), the *King James Version* (KJV), and *The Living Bible* (TLB). The 1984 NIV is the primary reference. (You will see minor wording differences if you are using an older version of the NIV translation.) When the other versions are used, they are identified by the above abbreviations.

Ideally, each school-aged child should have his or her own Bible. Any translation will do. In fact, a variety will make the lessons more interesting.

Colored pencils

Children will learn how to color-code Bible verses. Purchase quality colored pencils (soft lead) so that Bible pages will not tear. I recommend one set per person for maximum enjoyment and efficiency.

Yarn or narrow ribbon

Each person will need four pieces of narrow ribbon or yarn, twelve to fourteen inches long. These will be used as bookmarks, dividing the Bible into five sections. I suggest putting the ribbons at these locations: 1 Kings 1, Proverbs 1, Matthew 1, and Romans 1. If you purchase the ribbons, buy four colors. This will assist in locating Scriptures and help children learn general locations of the books of the Bible.

Pencils and an eraser

A quality eraser will actually erase colored pencil marks in the Bible.

Dictionary

Index cards

Included in this study are several methods involving index cards, to help make memorizing Scriptures fun.

IDEAS FOR CONDUCTING THE SESSION

Atmosphere

Make it a casual, happy experience. Sit around a table; it provides closeness as well as a surface for writing and color-coding Bible verses. Be alert for waning attention of younger children. Do not require them to color-code all the verses. You want your children to enjoy learning from the Bible.

Participation

Involvement is important. Let children assist in the planning. Everyone should have something to do at every session. Stress *cooperation* rather than *competition,* teamwork rather than rivalry. Let each person participate according to his abilities. Here are some suggestions:

1. Share events that happened or insights received since the last session.
2. Recite memorized verses.
3. Read the chapter title and key verse.

4. Share in reading the lesson or story; become a character in a play.
5. Locate the Scripture verses.
6. Read the verse aloud (others follow in their Bibles). If you have a variety of versions, let others read from their Bibles. Talk about different words used.
7. Discuss questions. Everyone should be encouraged to participate. Be sensitive to your children when they are willing to reveal their feelings and thoughts. Don't criticize. This is an opportunity to understand family members.
8. Act as family or group recorder, filling in the blanks or completing an activity.
9. Color-code the Bible verses with the proper colored pencil.
10. Read or create the closing prayer.
11. Allow younger children to be a part of the family unit by providing Bible coloring books.
12. Watch for opportunities to praise one another.

COLOR-CODING BIBLE VERSES

What is color-coding?
It is a simple method of marking a Bible to identify selected subjects. Most children enjoy this activity, but if you want to skip color-coding, that's okay. It takes time, but has some rich rewards.

Why color Bible verses?
1. It gives depth and purpose to Bible study. The reader must meditate upon or analyze a verse in order to choose the proper color. Verses often require more than one color.
2. It helps the reader understand where basic topics are concentrated.
3. It enables the reader to select one subject for review during a meditation time.
4. It preserves years of study, making the Bible personal and precious to its owner.
5. It aids in memorizing verses and their references.

PLANNING YOUR FIRST SESSION

In your first time together, your family will want to become acquainted with the project. To help you, the next section, "Getting Started," will take you step-by-step through this process.

Each child will learn according to ability. If you provide the opportunity, God will bless your efforts. Let the Holy Spirit be the teacher. Trust Him to give insight to your children as you study together. Ask God to guide you. Then relax and have fun with your family.

INTRODUCING THE PROJECT

When you travel, does your family ever play the alphabet game, "I'm going to grandmother's house, and I'm going to take . . ."? The first person completes that sentence with some object that begins with an A, like apples. The second person repeats the sentence with the A word and adds a B word. The third person adds a C word. Each family member participates in turn until the alphabet is complete. Of course, the game becomes harder as you get nearer the end of the alphabet. It's fun to see how much you can remember.

This book, *Learning About God . . . From A to Z,* is like playing that game. You're going to learn about the character of God from twenty-six words in alphabetical order. These words are attributes. They describe who God is, what He is like, and what He has done.

In 2 Peter 1:2-4 (TLB) you can read how important it is to learn about God:

Do you want more and more of God's kindness and peace? Then learn to know him better and better. For as you know him better, he will give you, through his great power, everything you need for living a truly good life: he even shares his own glory and his own goodness with us! And by that same mighty power he has given us all the other rich and wonderful blessings he promised.

To learn to know God better, you will be acting in plays, working puzzles, searching for Bible verses, memorizing Scriptures, and coloring verses in your Bibles. Your family or group can have lots of fun with these activities. First, let's get acquainted with your Bibles.

GETTING FAMILIAR WITH YOUR BIBLES

Understanding how the Bible is organized

In the front of your Bible is the contents page. In most Bibles, the books are listed in order from Genesis to Revelation. In others, the list is in alphabetical order. Page numbers are often given for each book of the Bible. This is a good place to look when you need help in locating an unfamiliar book.

The Bible is divided into two parts. What are they called? What is each about? (Discussion: Old Testament—story of God and His people; New Testament—story of Jesus and His followers.) How many books are in each part? In all? (Old Testament, thirty-nine; New

Testament, twenty-seven; Bible, sixty-six. Children can count them if they do not know.)

Sharing unique features

There are many different translations or versions of the Holy Bible. Look in the front of yours and see if you can identify which version or translation you have. (Discussion.)

Do you have pictures or maps, charts or study helps? (Discussion: children share unique contents of their Bibles.)

Locating the colored ribbons

There are four different colored ribbons for each of you. (Distribute the ribbons or yarn now.) These will be bookmarks, dividing your Bible into five sections.

Let's choose one color for each section. This will help us in locating Scripture verses later. (Let the children determine which color to put at each location: 1 Kings 1, Proverbs 1, Matthew 1, Romans 1.)

COLOR-CODING YOUR BIBLES

One of the activities you will be doing for each session is marking Bible verses with colored pencils. Color-coding a Bible verse will help you understand its meaning. (Distribute pencils now.)

Coloring hints

1. Color slowly and softly, so the pages won't tear.
2. Hold the pencil parallel to the page, tipping it slightly. Color with the side of the point, going back and forth several times.
3. Lay an index card at the sides of the verse. Coloring up to the card keeps the margins neat.

Choosing your color code

First you need to talk about the colors you will use. It helps if the colors are selected meaningfully, in association with something—a symbol or emblem. Discuss the suggestions below.

- Purple—royalty: The attributes of God: who God is, what He is like, what He has done.
- Yellow—gold, valuable: Promises or rewards: what God will do for those who love and obey Him.
- Brown—earth, reality: Duties and responsibilities of Christians: how we should act and speak.
- Red—blood: Jesus Christ: who He is and what He has done.
- Blue—sky: Anything about Heaven.
- Green—growing, alive: Holy Spirit: who He is and how He helps us.

• Orange—warmth, cheer: Family relationships: children, husbands, wives.

Making reference cards

To help remember the color code, each person should use an index card to make a simplified version of the above chart (or colors chosen by your family or group). The children can color each category on the card, which becomes a handy reference.

On larger cards (or construction paper folded like a tent), print the books of the Bible with common abbreviations. Place this "tent card" in the center of the table during each session so the children can refer to it often.

Color-coding a psalm

Let's color-code a few verses for practice.

1. Locate the Scripture. Use your "tent" card or the contents in the front of your Bible.
2. Read the passage aloud.
3. Think about it. What does the verse say?
4. Decide which phrases should be color-coded. You don't have to color the entire verse.
5. Choose your colors thoughtfully. You might not always agree with other people.

For example, Psalm 100 (emphasis added) could be coded using the following colors:

brown—Make a joyful noise unto the LORD, all ye lands. Serve the LORD with gladness: come before his presence with singing. Know ye that

purple—the LORD he *is* God: *it is* he *that* hath made us, and not we ourselves;

brown—*we are* his people, and the sheep of his pasture. Enter into his gates with thanksgiving, *and* into his courts with praise: be thankful unto him, *and* bless his name.

purple—For the LORD *is* good; his mercy is everlasting; and his truth *endureth* to all generations.

If you want to color-code other passages, find these verses:

• Matthew 1:21 (red)
• Galatians 5:22 (green)
• Ephesians 6:1-2 (orange and yellow)

A
· · · · · · · · · · ·
GOD IS ALMIGHTY

O great and powerful God, whose name is the LORD Almighty, great are your purposes and mighty are your deeds.

Jeremiah 32:18-19

POWER UNLIMITED

No doubt you have seen Superman leap over tall buildings, fly through the air, and crush trains and trucks. But he is only a make-believe character. No human has such strength or ability; only Almighty God has unlimited supernatural powers.

What do you think of when you hear the word *power* or *supernatural* or *almighty*? Each family member should fill in at least one blank and talk about it.

_____   _____   _____

_____   _____   _____

_____   _____   _____

Understanding words

God is almighty. *Almighty* means: He who controls or holds on to everything.

God is omnipotent (ahm-nip'-eh-tent). *Omni* means: all or completely; *potent* means: powerful or able. Putting these together, the word *omnipotent* means: God is all powerful, or God is completely able.

God has supreme power over everyone and everything, everywhere. Now that's unlimited power!

WHO SAID THAT?

Using five of your colored pencils, draw a line from each reference to its matching quotation. Draw another line from the quotation to the correct speaker. The quotations are from the *New International Version,* but you will recognize them in any Bible. (Remember to color these verses purple in your Bible.)

	QUOTATION	SPEAKER
Job 42:2	Abraham believed that "God had power to do what he had promised."	*Moses*
Jeremiah 32:27	"I know that you can do all things; no plan of yours can be thwarted."	*Paul*
Mark 10:27	"With man this is impossible, but not with God; all things are possible with God."	*Job*
Romans 4:20-21	"Great and marvelous are your deeds, LORD God Almighty."	*God*
Revelation 15:3	"Is anything too hard for me?"	*Jesus*

WHAT CAN GOD DO?

1. David wrote in Psalm 77:14, "You are the God who performs _____; you display your _____ among the peoples."

2. In Job 5:9 we read, "He performs _____ that cannot be fathomed, _____ that cannot be counted."

WHAT IS A MIRACLE?

Write a definition of a miracle below in your own words. If you need help, consult a dictionary.

_____

_____

_____

What's the secret message?

Miracles prove God's power over other gods and objects, people and nations, animals and nature, disease and death.

Read the Scriptures in the *New International Version* to find out what God had power over. Fill in the spaces. Transfer the numbered letters to the boxes with matching numbers in the puzzle below to discover a message about God.

1. Exodus 7:3 __ __ __ R __ __ __ ' __ __ __ __ T
                 6   24   41   12   27

2. Exodus 10:13 __ __ S __ __ __ __ __
                       13   38 25

3. Exodus 12:12 __ __ __ __ __ __ G __ __ __
                  20 29   16   1 40

4. Exodus 14:25 __ __ __ R __ __ __ __ __ __ L __
                       36   32   3 23   42

5. Joshua 4:23-24 __ O __ __ __ __ __ V __ __
                      5 45 37   10   15

6. Joshua 21:44 __ __ E __ __ __
                  33   17

7. Joshua 24:17-18 __ __ __ I __ __ __
                     7 44   30

8. 2 Kings 4:32-35 __ __ __ __ Y __ __ __ __ __ A __
                          46   28 11   8   26

9. 2 Kings 5:11-14 __ __ P __ __ __ __
                     34   47 19

10. Job 12:10 __ V __ __ __ __ __ T __ __
                4   22   35   14 21

11. Jonah 1:4 __ __ L __ __ __ S __ __ __
                39 2   18   43 31   9

	1	2	3	4	5		6	7	8		9	10	11	12	13	
14	15	16		17	18		19	20	21	22		23	24	25	26	
				27	28	29		30	31		32	33	34			
35	36	37		38	39	40	41	42	43	44	7	45		46	47	21

2 Chronicles 20:6

CHALLENGE

Here's a play about David and Goliath from 1 Samuel 17-18. If your family or group is small, some people may have to read several parts. Each person could have one prop (a long stick to resemble a shepherd's staff for David) or wear special clothing.

God shares His power

David—youngest son of Jesse; a teenager who tended sheep in the hills of Bethlehem

Jesse—an elderly father of eight sons

Eliab—oldest son and a soldier in Saul's army

Abinadab—second son and a soldier

Shammah—third son and a soldier

Goliath—a giant in the enemy Philistine army

Soldier—messenger from the king

Saul—king of Israel

Narrator—storyteller who describes action between scenes

Scene 1—A field outside Bethlehem

Narrator: When the story opens, David is on the hillside guarding his sheep. He is playing a flute when his father approaches.

Jesse: David, my son, how are the sheep?

David: Last night I had real trouble. A vicious lion attacked the sheep from that cliff. He grabbed one, but God gave me power to kill the lion and save the lamb. See, Father, under the rocks is the carcass of the lion.

Jesse: God is certainly with you.

David: Why have you come out here, Father? Is anything wrong?

Jesse: (anxious) Yes, Son. I'm worried about the war with the Philistines. We haven't heard from your three brothers for a long time. I want you to go to the battlefield and see if all is well.

David: (excited) Great! When do I go?

Jesse: Tomorrow. I want you to take some roasted corn and ten loaves of bread to your brothers. And I want to send some cheese to their captain.

David: Oh, I love to go to the battlefield and see the soldiers. I wish I were old enough to fight.

A²¹

Jesse: That day will come soon enough. Hurry now. Go ask your friend to watch the flock while you're gone.

Narrator: Early the next morning, David put the supplies in a backpack and set out for the battlefield. He hiked over the mountains and into the Valley of Elah where Saul's army was camped.

Scene 2—On the battlefield

Narrator: When David arrived, the two armies were forming their battle lines, facing each other. David left his pack with the keeper of supplies and ran to find his brothers.

David: (calling) Shammah! Abinadab!

Shammah: Brother, what are you doing here?

David: I bring greetings and food from Father. Are you safe? Who's winning the war?

Abinadab: We're safe. But we're *not* winning. Look over yonder (pointing to Goliath).

Goliath: (shouting) Why do you soldiers line up for battle? Do you need a whole army to settle this war? Send someone to fight me (strutting, pounding his chest). If your man kills me, the Philistines will be your slaves. But if I kill him, you must be our slaves.

David: Who is this Philistine soldier? Why do we let him insult the armies of the living God? (surprised) And why are our soldiers running away?

Shammah: Goliath is a giant of a man, David. He's almost ten feet tall. Everyone is afraid of him.

David: Everyone?

Abinadab: He wears a bronze helmet and leggings. His armored coat alone weighs two hundred pounds.

Goliath: (shouting arrogantly) I challenge the armies of Israel. Send out a man who will fight.

David: Won't anyone go?

Shammah: David, you don't understand. His javelin is several inches thick; its iron tip weighs twenty-five pounds.

Abinadab: See the huge shield carried by his armor bearer. What chance would any of us have?

David: How long has this been going on?

Shammah: Forty days. Every morning and every night that giant struts across the mountaintop, shouting insults at us. For forty days our army has been retreating in fear.

Abinadab: (sadly) No one is brave enough to face Goliath. King Saul is getting desperate.

Shammah: The king offers great wealth to the man who kills Goliath. That man will marry the king's daughter, and his family will never have to pay taxes again.

David: Surely, there is someone who . . .

Eliab: (Enters, angrily) What are you doing here, David? You should be home tending the sheep. I know what a rascal you are. What excuses did you give Father so you could come and watch the battle?

David: What have I done to make you so angry? Can't I even ask questions or say what I think?

Soldier: Pardon me for interrupting, but King Saul requests that David come to his tent.

Scene 3—In King Saul's tent

Narrator: At the tent door, David bowed to the king.

Saul: David, soldiers have heard you talking boldly about the Philistine giant.

David: That's right, O king, and you don't have to worry about anything. I, your servant, will fight him.

Saul: Don't joke with me, David. How can a shepherd boy fight with a powerful and experienced warrior?

David: A shepherd protects his sheep. When wild animals attacked my flock, I used my club to beat them. I saved the lambs right out of their mouths. Once I killed a bear. Last week I killed a lion.

Saul: The Philistine is far more dangerous than a lion or a bear.

David: The *Lord* saved me from the claws of the lion and the bear. I know He will save me from the hand of this Philistine.

Saul: If you insist, I won't stop you. However, you must wear my helmet and coat of armor.

A²³

Narrator: David obeyed the king. He put on the armor, strapped the sword over it, and tried to walk around the tent.

David: I can't wear these. I can hardly move.

Saul: Without soldier's equipment, how will you kill this giant?

David: I'll use the weapon I'm most familiar with and trust God to give me power.

Saul: (prayerfully) May God go with you.

Narrator: David took off the king's armor and left the tent.

Scene 4—In the valley

Narrator: From a nearby stream, David picked up five smooth stones and put them into his leather pouch. Carrying his staff, he ran across the valley.

Goliath: (laughing with hate) Am I a dog that a boy comes to fight me with a stick? By the gods of the Philistines, I curse you.

David: (shouting) You come to me with a sword and a spear. But I come to you in the name of the Lord Almighty, the God of the armies of Israel whom you have insulted.

Goliath: Come here! I'll feed your body to the birds and the bears.

David: Today the Lord will give me power to conquer you.

Narrator: David hurled a stone from his sling. The stone hit the Philistine squarely in the forehead, and the giant fell to the ground. David ran and stood over him. Clutching Goliath's sword, David cut off the giant's head.

David: (shouting to the Philistines) This battle was not won with a sword or a spear, but by the power of our God. (shouting to the Israelites) Today, the world will know there is no other god like the God of Israel.

□　　□　　□

Discussion

1. Why wasn't David afraid of the giant? (See 1 Samuel 17:37,45.)

2. Why was David able to kill the giant? (See 1 Samuel 16:13.)

3. God shares His power when people trust and obey Him. What Bible characters can you think of to whom God gave His power?

☆ APPLICATION

1. a. When have you ever done something difficult and then wondered how you did it?

   b. From whom were you given extra power and strength?

2. Discuss how God's power can help you live a better Christian life in the home, at work, at school, during sports, during dating, when witnessing.

PRAYER

Almighty God,
we are amazed at Your mighty power
and that You are willing to share it
with people who love You.
Please strengthen us through Your Holy Spirit
so that we can obey Your Word.
Although we cannot understand it,
help us to believe that Your great power
will be given to us if we trust in You.
In Jesus' name, amen.

B

· · · · · · · · · · · · · ·

GOD IS THE BLESSING-GIVER

"Test me in this," says the LORD Almighty, "and see if I will not throw open the floodgates of heaven and pour out so much blessing that you will not have room enough for it."

Malachi 3:10

B

UNDERSTANDING BLESSINGS

Can you define a blessing?

1. Talk about these questions. Then check the correct box.

	YES	NO
a. Is a blessing something that brings you happiness?	☐	☐
b. Is it something to be afraid of?	☐	☐
c. Is it something that improves your situation?	☐	☐
d. Is it something you can earn or buy?	☐	☐
e. Is it a kind deed or a gift from God?	☐	☐

God gives two kinds of blessings: physical and spiritual.

2. Fill in the blanks to find examples of these blessings.
   Paul wrote that the living God "has shown kindness by giving

   you _____ from heaven and _____ in their

   seasons; he provides you with plenty of _____ and fills

   your _____ with _____" (Acts 14:17).

Can you touch a blessing?

Some of God's blessings are *tangible* (can be touched); some are *intangible* (cannot be touched).

3. God gave Solomon five wonderful blessings. To identify them read 2 Chronicles 1:12.

   a. Tangible: _____, _____

   b. Intangible: _____, _____, _____

Can you receive a blessing?

4. Read Psalm 115:12-13 and fill in the blanks to find out if you can receive a blessing: "The LORD remembers us and will bless us. . . .

   He will bless those who _____ the LORD—

   _____ and _____ alike."

Can you find a blessing?

Have you ever gone on a scavenger hunt? When you play this game, the leader gives everyone a list of unusual items. As teams, you knock on neighbor's doors, asking for these items. The first team to collect all the items is the winner.

Let's go on a "blessing hunt." Below is a list of Scripture verses. Can you find the blessings? As a family or separate teams, look up one verse at a time, talk about it, and fill in the chart. (To help locate the verses, put your tent-card of the books of the Bible on the table.) To color-code these verses, you will need purple, yellow, and brown.

The blessing hunt

GOD'S BLESSINGS	TO WHOM
Genesis 26:12-14	
Genesis 39:2-3	
Deuteronomy 16:15	
Job 1:8-10	
Psalm 29:11	
Psalm 84:11-12	
Ezekiel 34:26-27	
Ephesians 1:3	

Counting Abraham's blessings

Abraham received many blessings from God. Complete this puzzle to identify some of them. The clues include verses in Genesis if you need help.

ABRAHAM'S

B __ __
L __ __ __
__ E __ __ __ __ __ __
__ S __ __ __ __ __ __
S __ __ __ __
__ I __ __ __ __ __ __ __
N __ __ __ __ __ __ __
__ __ __ G __
__ __ __ S __ __ __ __ __

Clues

Male child; son

Property (13:15)

Workers and slaves (24:34-35)

_____ and gold (24:35)

Lambs (24:35)

Cattle (13:2)

Father of many _____ (17:5)

Male rulers (17:6)

Children (13:15)

☆APPLICATION

The rain falls and the sun shines on both the birds and the rocks. The birds chirp their thanks for the warm sunlight and the refreshing rain. The rocks do nothing. Because they have no feeling, they do not appreciate the sun or rain.

Blessings all around us go unnoticed and unappreciated every day. Are you like the birds or the rocks? Talk about some blessings you might have taken for granted (example: good eyesight).

CHALLENGE

John 1:16 says, "From the fullness of his grace we have all received one blessing after another." In an old hymn we are reminded to "Count Your Blessings."

Start a "blessing list." Write down your blessings, great or small. Or make a family chart and post it on a door. During the week, everyone can write down blessings received.

BLESSINGS OF THE _____ **FAMILY**

Tangible   **Intangible**

PRAYER

O Lord,
You are so good and kind.
I'm happy to know You enjoy helping us.
Thank You for the blessings You have given our family.
It's really surprising how many there are,
but we just didn't recognize them.
Forgive us for taking them for granted.
Please make us more aware of Your blessings.
And, Lord, help us to be grateful for every blessing You send,
whether it is big or small.
In Jesus' name, amen.

C

· · · · · · · · · · · ·

GOD IS OUR CREATOR

"Sovereign Lord . . . you made the heaven and the earth and the sea, and everything in them."

Acts 4:24

CREATOR OF EVERYTHING

The first chapter of Genesis tells how our world began. You will be part of a "speaking choir" as you read this story.

How our world began
Genesis 1

Reader 1—the narrator
Reader 2—voice of God
Boys—can be one or many
Girls—can be one or many
All—the entire family or class

Reader 1: In the beginning, God created the heavens and the earth. The earth was empty and without form. Darkness and water were everywhere.

Girls: And God said,

Reader 2: Let there be light.

Boys: And there was light.

Reader 1: God was pleased with the light. He separated the light from the darkness.

Girls: God called the light "day."

Boys: God called the darkness "night."

All: This happened on the first day.

Girls: And God said,

Reader 2: Let there be space between the waters.

Boys: And it was so.

Reader 1: God made space. He separated the water under space from the water above space.

Girls: God called the space "sky."

All: This happened on the second day.

Girls: And God said,

Reader 2: Let the water under the sky be gathered together, and let dry ground appear.

Boys: And it was so.

Girls: God called the dry ground "land."

Boys: God called the gathered waters "seas."

Reader 1: God was pleased with the land and seas He had made.

Girls: And God said,

Reader 2: Let plants and trees grow on this land. And let the plants and trees have flowers, vegetables, and fruit upon them. And let them have seeds so they can produce more plants and trees.

Boys: And it was so.

Reader 1: The land produced many grasses, plants, and trees with seeds according to their kind.

Girls: And God saw that it was good.

All: This happened on the third day.

Girls: And God said,

Reader 2: Let there be lights in the sky to separate the day from the night. These lights will determine the days and months, seasons and years.

Boys: And it was so.

Reader 1: God made two great lights—

Girls: The sun to rule the day;

Boys: The moon to rule the night.

Reader 1: He also made millions of stars.

Girls: And God saw that it was good.

All: This happened on the fourth day.

Girls: And God said,

Reader 2: Let living creatures swim in the waters. Let birds fly in the sky.

Reader 1: So God created the fish and creatures of the seas. He created every winged bird that flies in the air.

C 35

Girls: And God saw that it was good.

Boys: God blessed them and said,

Reader 2: Be healthy and multiply. Fill the seas and the skies with your babies.

All: This happened on the fifth day.

Girls: And God said,

Reader 2: Let the land be filled with living creatures: tame animals, wild animals, and creatures that move along the ground.

Boys: And it was so.

Reader 1: God made wild animals, livestock, and crawling creatures, each according to its kind.

Girls: And God saw that it was good. Then God said,

Reader 2: Let Us make man—human beings—in Our image, like Ourselves. Let them rule over all life upon the earth, in the skies, and in the seas.

Reader 1: So God created man like Himself. In the image of God, He made people. He made both male and female.

Boys: God blessed them and said to them,

Reader 2: Be happy and healthy and have a family. Fill the earth with your offspring. Rule over everything I have made.

Girls: And it was so.

Boys: God looked at all that He had created.

Girls: And it was *very* good.

All: This happened on the sixth day.

Reader 1: And now the heavens and earth were successfully completed. God's creation was perfect in every way.

All: On the seventh day, God rested.

❑   ❑   ❑

What God made and when

Open your Bible to Genesis 1. You may want to color-code the verses that tell us God is the great Creator.

WHAT GOD MADE	WHEN
Genesis 1:1	
1:3-4	
1:7	
1:9-10	
1:11	
1:14,16	
1:21	
1:25	
1:27	

HOW GOD CREATED THE WORLD

1. In Jeremiah 10:12 we read, "But God made the earth by his

   _____; he founded the world by his _____

   and stretched out the heavens by his _____."

2. David wrote in Psalm 33:6,9 (TLB), "He _____, and the heavens were formed, and all the galaxies of stars. . . . For when

   he but _____, the world began. It appeared at his

   _____."

☆ APPLICATION

Read Psalm 95:3-7. How should we respond to God, our Maker? Why? (You can color-code this passage with purple and brown.)

CHALLENGE

Memorizing Scripture: *Method 1—Colored Words*

1. Each person should copy a key verse (or another of his choice

from this chapter) on an index card. With a regular pencil, print lightly in large letters. Include the reference.

2. Find all the names for God and the pronouns that stand for God. With a purple pencil, trace over these words.
3. Find all the nouns (name of a person, place, or thing). Trace over the letters in each noun with the red pencil.
4. Find all the verbs (action words). Outline the letters with the green pencil.
5. Are there any pronouns that mean *you*? Trace over these words with the orange pencil.
6. With your black pencil, trace over the letters of all the remaining words.
7. Tape the card to a mirror in your bedroom or bathroom.
8. Read it every morning and every night for one week.

The children will become familiar with the verse and its meaning as they do each of the first six steps. By reading it daily, they will soon have it memorized.

If you elect to do this with one verse for each chapter, your family or class will know twenty-six verses about the attributes of God by the time you complete this book. (You can also choose verses from chapters A and B.)

PRAYER

O God,
You are a wonderful and wise Creator.
Thank You for making this beautiful world for us to enjoy.
Thank You for making us in Your own image.
We will never forget that You are the Creator of man,
and that only Almighty God could perform such a miracle.
Remind us of Your mighty power
when we see a snowflake fall,
or feel the warmth of the sun,
or hear the laughter of a friend.
In Jesus' name, amen.

D

GOD IS OUR DELIVERER

The LORD is my rock, and my
fortress, and my deliverer; my God,
my strength, in whom I will trust.

Psalm 18:2, KJV

D³⁹

WHAT IS A DELIVERER?

A *deliverer* is a person:

- who *sets free* or *releases* someone from slavery, prison, or suffering;
- who *rescues* or *saves* another from danger, capture, or death.

Real rescuers

In some occupations, men and women rescue other people. Sometimes they even risk their own lives as they save others. Choose the right person from the list below and fill in each blank.

1. _____ Rescues a baby from a burning building.

2. _____ Saves a child from drowning in a lake.

3. _____ Releases an innocent man from prison.

4. _____ Saves an injured person through surgery.

5. _____ Frees a hostage by capturing a criminal.

6. _____ Rescues lost hikers and hunters.

7. _____ Saves a friend by giving first aid.

8. _____ Rushes emergency patients to a hospital.

Search and rescue team
Doctor
Judge
Boy scout
Fireman
Policeman
Life guard
Paramedic

Fictional rescuers

Make-believe rescuers come in all shapes and sizes, from Mighty Mouse to Robin Hood. See if you can name some deliverers and rescuers from literature and television.

There are many rescuers—both real and imaginary—in our world today. But the Scriptures tell us that God is the greatest Deliverer.

THE GREATEST RESCUER

A reliable reporter must answer the five W questions: Who? What? When? Where? Why? We'll add one more: HoW? Let's look in the Bible to find the answers about God, the greatest Rescuer. (Don't forget to color-code these verses.)

1. *Who* is the Great Rescuer?

   a. Read Daniel 3:28. When three young men were saved from the fiery furnace, King Nebuchadnezzar said, "Praise be to _____

   _____

   b. Read Daniel 3:29. "No other god _____

   _____

2. *What* does the Great Rescuer deliver people from?

   Psalm 34:4 _____

   Psalm 34:17 _____

3. *When* does God deliver people?

   Psalm 22:4 _____

   Jonah 2:1-2 _____

4. *Where* does God deliver people?

   Daniel 3:17 _____

   Jonah 2:10 _____

5. *Why* does God deliver people?

   Psalm 18:19 _____

   Psalm 91:14 _____

6. *How* does God deliver His people?

   Joshua 10:11 _____

   Acts 12:11 _____

CHALLENGE

The following play is similar to the popular television news show "Good Morning, America."

Get aboard the time machine with the television reporter and camera crew from BBS (Bible Broadcasting System). We're going to travel back through the time tunnel to 541 BC to the palace of King Darius in Babylon.

Good Morning, Babylon
Daniel 6:1-28

Chris Kelly—BBS reporter
King Darius—ruler of Babylon
Daniel—a manager or officer for King Darius
A satrap—(say' trap) like a governor

Chris: (looking into the camera) Good morning, Babylon. Today is Friday, 541 BC. Exciting things have been happening in Babylon. Everyone is talking about how Daniel, a manager for King Darius, was rescued from the lions' den. Here to tell us the facts are King Darius—whose own law began it all—Daniel, and one of the satraps serving under Daniel. And I'm Chris Kelly, your BBS reporter.

(turning to the king) King Darius, you ordered your soldiers to arrest Daniel. Then you had him thrown into the lions' den. Yet you rejoiced the next morning when he was still alive. This sounds like a riddle to me.

Darius: Actually, I was tricked. I admire Daniel very much. He has unusual wisdom and ability. He's my best manager.

Chris: Daniel, how do you feel about that compliment?

Daniel: My wisdom and ability are gifts from God. I give all the credit to Him for whatever I have done in Babylon.

Chris: That's very humble of you, but I understand you are eighty years old. That's a lot of living—a lot of experience.

Daniel: That's true. I was sixteen when Jerusalem fell under the attack of King Nebuchadnezzar. I was among the first captives brought here to Babylon. For sixty-five years, I have tried to honor and faithfully serve the kings of Babylon.

Darius: Daniel is respected by all the people.

Chris: Obviously not by everyone. Someone wanted Daniel killed.

Satrap: More than one person. The other two managers hated Daniel because he was getting all the attention and honors. In fact, we heard a rumor that King Darius was going to make Daniel president over the entire kingdom. This meant that everyone would be under Daniel's control.

Chris: What did the jealous leaders do?

Satrap: At first, they searched for some fault in the way Daniel managed his area. They planned to complain to the king so Daniel wouldn't get the promotion. But Daniel is so wise and honest the managers couldn't find a single mistake. Finally one of them said, "Our only chance is to attack his religion. He worships the Hebrew God instead of the gods of Babylon."

Darius: A committee came to me and said: "King Darius, live forever! All the managers and satraps of your kingdom have agreed. . . ."

Satrap: (interrupting) That was a lie! We did not *all* agree.

Darius: But, I didn't know that. They said to me, "O noble king, we believe you should make a law, that for the next thirty days anyone who prays to any god or man, except to you, shall be thrown into the lions' den."

Chris: And did you agree to that?

Darius: It sounded like a good idea. All kings like power and praise. I'm no different.

Chris: So you signed that law. According to the strict rules of the Medes and Persians, it can never be changed. Is that true?

Darius: A law cannot be changed even by the one who signs it.

Chris: Daniel, you ignored this law. You went right on praying publicly three times a day to your own God. Why—when you knew you would face death in a den of hungry lions?

Daniel: No king, no law, no lions can come between me and my God.

Satrap: Everyone knew how faithful Daniel was to his God. The managers sent spies to watch Daniel. As soon as Daniel went to his room and knelt to pray, the spies reported it to the managers.

Chris: What did the managers tell you, King Darius?

D⁴³

Darius: A committee came to me and reminded me of the law I had signed and that it could not be changed. Then the leader said, "Someone has disobeyed your law, O king." "Who?" I asked. He replied, "Daniel, one of the Jewish captives. He refuses to bow before your statue. He still prays three times a day to his God."

Chris: So you were trapped?

Darius: I was trapped. I was mad! I was sad! I didn't want Daniel killed. He was too valuable to me. I tried to think of a way to save Daniel, but there was none.

Chris: Daniel, tell us—what happened next?

Daniel: While I was praying, the soldiers came to my room and took me away like a dangerous criminal. When we reached the entrance to the lions' den, King Darius was there. He looked at me and said quietly, "Daniel, may your God, whom you serve faithfully, rescue you." Then he ordered the soldiers to throw me into the cave.

Satrap: After the soldiers pushed Daniel into the cave, they rolled a big boulder into the opening. They poured hot wax into the cracks around the boulder. Then the king pressed his ring into the wax to seal it. This meant no one could rescue Daniel.

Darius: I went right to my palace. I couldn't eat. I sent the singers and jugglers away. I couldn't sleep. All night long I worried about Daniel.

Chris: Has anyone ever escaped from the lions before?

Darius: Never! The lions are so hungry they immediately attack anything thrown into the den.

Chris: Then why did you worry or wonder about Daniel? Didn't you believe your lions would eat him?

Darius: I hoped that his God was as great as Daniel claimed He was. I hoped, oh, how I hoped, his God could save him somehow.

Chris: Daniel, what happened during the night?

Daniel: When the soldiers pushed me into the cave, I stumbled and fell. Roaring lions surrounded me. When they came within a foot, they stopped as if an invisible wall stood between us. They quit roaring, laid down near my feet, and went to sleep.

Chris: What did you do then?

Daniel: I knelt and prayed. I thanked God for protecting me. Then I slept. Early in the morning, I heard a voice calling my name. I looked up through the opening in the roof of the cave, and there stood the king.

Darius: I was afraid to look down, so I just called, "Daniel, Daniel, servant of the living God, are you there? Was your God whom you worship able to deliver you from the lions?" Then I heard Daniel's voice, "Your Majesty, live forever!" What a relief! When I looked down, I saw Daniel with the lions sitting at his feet.

Chris: How do you explain this, Daniel?

Daniel: My God sent His angel to shut the lions' mouths. They did not hurt me because I was innocent before God. And I have never done any wrong before King Darius either.

Darius: Immediately I ordered my soldiers to lift Daniel out of the den. I looked over his body. There wasn't a single scratch on him. His clothing wasn't even torn.

Daniel: That's because I trusted God to deliver me.

Darius: I was happy that Daniel was alive. But I was angry with those who had tricked me, so I commanded that they be killed.

Chris: How?

Satrap: Let me tell this part. The soldiers found the men who had accused Daniel and brought them to the king. Daniel's enemies were thrown into the lions' den. The lions leaped into the air and grabbed the bodies before they reached the ground.

Darius: That was proof enough for me that the Almighty God had saved Daniel's life.

Chris: (looking into the camera) What an incredible rescue! What a testimony for the God of Daniel.

BBS wishes to thank King Darius, Daniel, and the satrap for sharing this experience with the people of Babylon. This is Chris Kelly saying goodbye from Good Morning, Babylon.

Darius: *Wait!*

Chris: (turning to the king) Is there more?

D⁴⁵

Darius: Yes, I have written a new law, and I want to read it to my people. (King stands and faces the camera.) "I command that in every part of my kingdom people must respect and honor the God of Daniel. For his God is the living, unchanging God. His kingdom can never be destroyed and His power shall never end. He saves His people from harm. He delivered Daniel from the power of the lions."

Chris: I'm sure all our listeners will agree with you, King Darius, that Daniel's God is the true God and the great Deliverer.

□   □   □

Discussion

1. What method did God use to save Daniel from the lions?

2. Daniel said there were two reasons why the lions did not eat him. What were they?

☆ APPLICATION

God still rescues people today, but they often fail to recognize His miracles. Talk about times when God rescued you or your family. Don't say, "It happened accidentally," or "I was lucky," or "It was just a coincidence."

Geometric code

Below is something important to remember about God, the Deliverer. To read this secret-code message, write the correct letter above each geometric symbol.

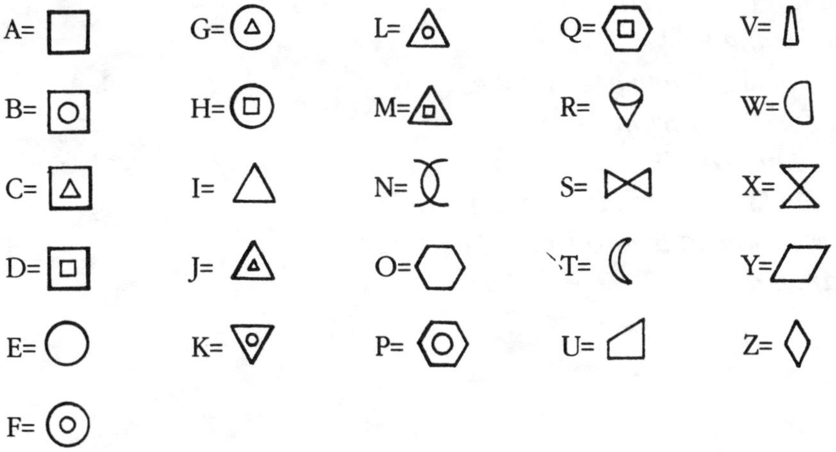

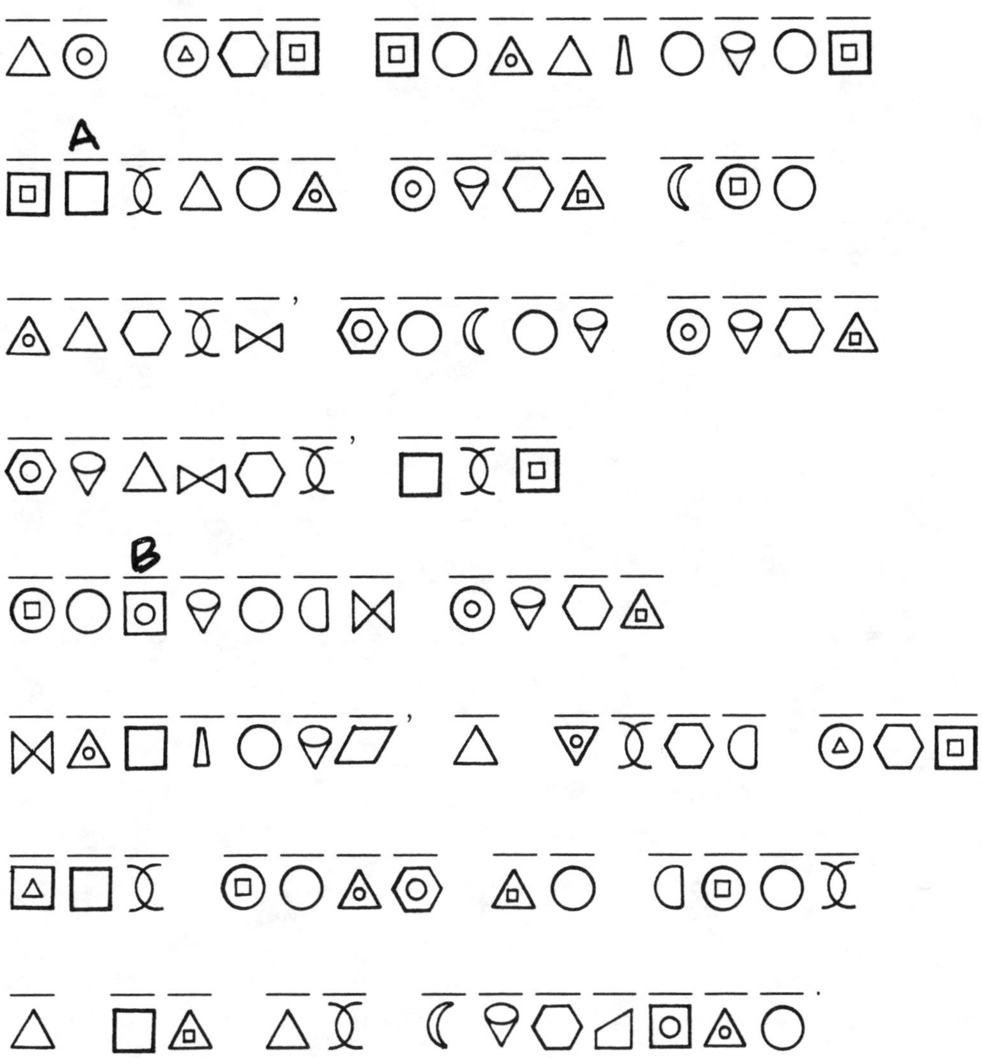

PRAYER

Dear God,
You are powerful,
able to rescue in any situation.
Nothing is too hard for You, O Lord.
Thank You for the Bible
that tells us how You delivered people.
Thank You for Your promises
to help me when I am in trouble.
I know You will rescue me if I obey Your Word.
Lord, teach me how to live so I may please You.
In Jesus' name, amen.

E

· · · · · · · · · · · · ·

GOD IS
ETERNAL

But the LORD is the true God; he is
the living God, the eternal King.

Jeremiah 10:10

NO BEGINNING, NO ENDING

"What time is it?" Bret pulls his green jersey, number 20, over his head.

"It's 1:30!" his sister yells up the stairs. "If you don't hurry, you'll miss your own soccer game."

□　　□　　□

"Today is June 21, first day of summer," announces Mother. "Tomorrow we begin our vacation."

Jennifer packs her purple-striped bathing suit. "Ten days at the beach. I can hardly wait."

□　　□　　□

Clocks and calendars control our lives. They help us keep track of time. Time! Everyone's concerned about time because everything we do has a beginning and an ending. A soccer game, a school year, spring season, summer vacation, shopping trips, Sunday sermons, chores, and wars.

What about people? We have beginnings and endings, too. We are born and we die.

OPPOSITES DESCRIBE GOD

Have you ever played the "Game of Opposites"? One person says a word and someone names its opposite. For example: I say "up," you say "down." Then you think of something these opposites represent. "up-down" might make you think "elevator." There's no wrong answer. Each person may have a different idea.

OPPOSITES		ASSOCIATION
UP	DOWN	ELEVATOR
Beginning		
Start		
	Closing	
First		
Introduction		
Front		
Birth		
	Grave	
	Z	
Alpha		
	Sunset	
Entrance		

Some of these opposites are used in Scripture to describe God. They tell us God is eternal—everlasting.

1. In Isaiah 44:6 we read, "This is what the LORD says . . . 'I am the

   _____ and I am the _____; apart from me there is no God.'"

2. God describes Himself in Revelation 1:8 (KJV): "'I am

   _____ and _____, the _____ and the

   _____,' saith the Lord, 'which _____, and

   which _____, and which _____, the Almighty.'"

UNDERSTANDING WORDS

God is eternal. That means He is without a beginning or ending. God lived before creation; He lives now; and He will live forever. He is immortal; He cannot die.

If you look up the word *eternal* in the dictionary, you'll find definitions like *timeless, ageless, limitless, endless.* Because human beings are born and die and because everything we do has a beginning and an ending, it's hard to understand how God can be eternal.

Let's talk about timeless, ageless, and endless. The suffix *-less* on the end of a word means *without* something. So timeless means *without time.* What does ageless mean? Endless?

God is timeless.

1. David wrote in Psalm 93:2, "Your throne was established

   _____; you are from _____."

2. In 2 Peter 3:8 we read, "But do not forget this one thing, dear

   friends: With the Lord a _____ is like a _____

   _____, and a _____ _____ are like a

   _____."

God is ageless.

3. We learn from Job 36:26: "How great is God—beyond our

   understanding! The number of his years is

   _____."

4. In Psalm 102:27, David wrote of God, "But you remain the same,

   and your years _____."

God is endless.

5. Paul wrote to Timothy, "Now to the King _____,

   _____, invisible, the only God, be honor and glory

   _____ and _____" (1 Timothy 1:17).

6. We can draw comfort from Isaiah 40:7-8: "Surely the people are grass. The grass withers and the flowers fall, but the

   _____ of our God stands _____."

☆ APPLICATION

God is timeless, ageless, and endless; however, man's life is brief and fragile.

1. Read Psalm 90:2-6 (in *The Living Bible*).
   a. Compare God with man.

   b. What things in nature are used to illustrate man's short life?

2. Read Psalm 90:12.
   a. What does it mean to number our days?

   b. *The Living Bible* says, "Help us to spend them [days] as we should." This could be part of your prayer.

CHALLENGE

Color-code these verses about the everlasting God.

- 1 Chronicles 16:36
- Nehemiah 9:5
- Isaiah 40:28
- 1 Timothy 6:15-16

ETERNITY IS LIKE A CIRCLE

When you were younger, you probably played games like "Farmer in the Dell" or "Ring Around the Rosie." Everyone held hands, making a big circle. Was there a beginning or ending to the circle?

A wedding ring is a circle that has no starting place or stopping place. The ring goes round and round. Similarly, eternity goes on and on.

The following puzzle has three circles or rings; each ring has a secret message. In each ring, the first letter of the first word is also the last letter of the last word. Like eternity, each message just keeps going on and on.

To learn the secret messages, you must decipher the code. Fill in the code chart below as you discover letters in the puzzle. You only need sixteen letters of the alphabet. Four clues will help you get started.

1. G   5. __   9. __   13. __

2. __   6. __   10. __   14. __

3. E   7. A   11. __   15. __

4. __   8. N   12. __   16. __

God is eternal.

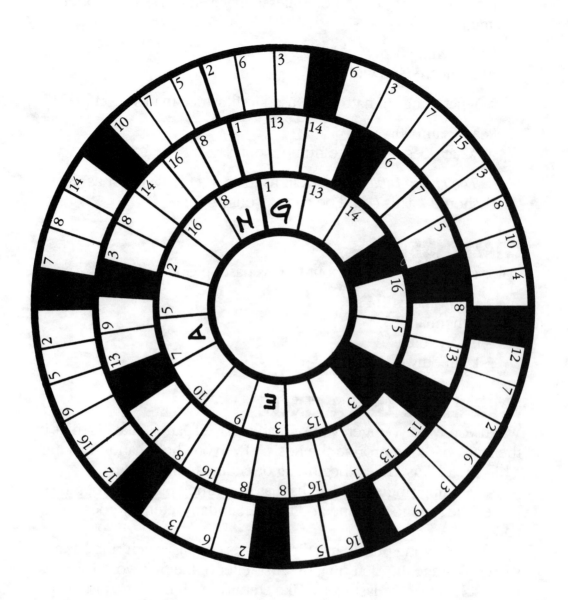

PRAYER

Dear God,
I know You created the world and everything in it.
But where did You come from?
It's hard to understand
how You can have no beginning and no ending.
It's also hard to understand the wind.
I can feel it when it's blowing.
But I don't understand where it comes from or where it goes.
I can plant a tiny seed in the earth.
But I don't understand how it becomes a tall shade tree.
I guess I don't have to understand something to believe it.
Help me believe You are eternal
because You told me so in the Bible.
In Jesus' name, amen.

F

· · · · · · · · · · · · ·

GOD IS OUR FATHER

I will be a Father to you, and you
will be my sons and daughters, says
the Lord Almighty.

2 Corinthians 6:18

F

MADE AND ADOPTED

"He is too," said eight-year-old Mark with a trembling voice.

"He is not," teased his older sister, Tammy.

"Yes, he is."

"No, he's not."

Mr. Ballard laid down his newspaper. "Maybe I can settle this argument. What's it all about?"

"Tammy said you're not my real father 'cuz I wasn't born to you and Mom like she was. She said being adopted doesn't count."

"Come here, both of you."

Tammy and Mark sat on the sofa beside their father.

"Eleven years ago, your mother and I wanted a baby very much. So together we made a baby, so to speak. She was born to us, and we named her Tammy Ballard. The hospital gave us papers that said she legally belonged to us.

"Two years later we wanted another baby, just as much as we wanted the first one. So Mother and I adopted a baby. We chose a boy, named him Mark Ballard, and signed papers that said he legally belonged to Mother and me.

"You both were wanted! You both have our family name. And you both are loved more than I can ever tell. Made or adopted, you both belong to me. I am your father."

Mr. Ballard hugged his son. "So you see, Mark, being adopted *does* count. It counts very much. Understand?"

Mark sniffled and nodded his head.

Mr. Ballard pinched Tammy's cheek. "And you, my little lady, will not tease your brother anymore. Agreed?"

"Agreed! Come on, *brother*, let's go play."

□   □   □

THE FAMILY OF GOD

God is our Father in two ways. First, He is our Father because He created us. Second, He is our Father because He adopted us when He redeemed us from sin.

1. Moses spoke these words: "Is he not your _____, your

_____, who _____ you and _____

you?" (Deuteronomy 32:6).

58F

2. Isaiah 64:8 says, "Yet, O LORD, you are our _____. We are the _____, you are the _____; we are all the _____ of your hand."

3. The prophet Malachi spoke God's message: "Have we not all one _____? Did not one God _____ us?" (Malachi 2:10).

Through creation, God has been the Father of everyone everywhere. And He longs to call everyone His son or daughter. But a person is not truly a part of the family of God until he or she accepts Jesus Christ as Savior.

We are His children.

4. How do we become children of God? Read these Scriptures and write the answer in your own words.

Matthew 12:50 _____

John 1:12 _____

Galatians 3:26 _____

As our heavenly Father, God is our nearest and dearest relative. He loves us more than we will ever know and wants to care for us in special ways.

Characteristics of our heavenly Father

5. After reading each Scripture, draw a line to the matching trait.

Psalm 103:13	Corrects and disciplines.
Proverbs 3:11-12	Pours out His incredible love.
Matthew 6:14	Is tender and kind.
Matthew 6:26	Believes His children are valuable.
2 Corinthians 6:16	Forgives disobedience.
1 John 3:1	Likes to be with His children.

Benefits of being God's children

6. After reading the Scripture, choose the best answer—the one you believe is described in that verse.
   a. Matthew 7:11—You will receive:
      ___ great riches   ___ good gifts   ___ food and clothes

   b. Ephesians 2:19—You will become:
      ___ popular   ___ famous   ___ part of God's family

   c. Romans 8:17—You will inherit:
      ___ treasures   ___ eternal life   ___ earthly blessings

☆ APPLICATION

1. What does *discipline* mean?

2. How do your parents discipline you?

3. Sometimes children think they aren't loved because their parents correct or punish them. Why do parents discipline their children? (See Proverbs 3:11-12, 22:6.)

4. Why does God discipline His children?

CHALLENGE

Memorizing Scripture: *Method 2—Scrambled Words*

1. Cut five index cards in half.

2. Choose a Scripture from the lesson and read it in unison several times. Let's use John 1:12 as an example.

3. Print two or more words on each card, making ten cards:
   Yet to all / who received him, / to those / who believed / in his name, / he gave / the right / to become / children of God. (John 1:12)

4. Mix the cards up in the middle of the table. Taking turns, let each family member put the cards in the proper order.

5. To make a game out of this method, choose another verse such as Ephesians 3:20. Make ten cards for this verse as follows:
   Now to him / who is able to do / immeasurably more / than all we ask / or imagine, / according to / his power / that is at work / within us.
   (Ephesians 3:20)

6. With a blue felt marker, draw a large X *on the back* of the cards for the first verse. With a red marker draw a circle on the back of all cards for the second verse.

7. Put the cards in the center of the table, words facing down.

8. Two people (or two teams) can play; one uses the blue X cards; the other, the red O. At a signal they gather their cards, turn them over, and see how quickly each can arrange the phrases in the proper order. The first player done is the winner. Everyone reads the verses to judge if they are correct.

9. Save these cards. Later, you can add new verses. Soon there will be enough so the entire family can play, each member using a separate verse.

Famous Bible families

In the following hidden word puzzle, you'll be looking for eight Bible families—fathers, mothers, sons—all listed. The words are spelled vertically, horizontally, diagonally, forwards, and backwards. Draw a line around each one.

Can you also find eight secret words associated with families? When you find them, fill in the blanks. If you need help, they are listed below the puzzle.

FATHERS	MOTHERS	SONS	SECRET WORDS
Adam	Eve	Abel	_____
Abraham	Sarah	Isaac	_____
Jacob	Rachel	Benjamin	_____
Boaz	Ruth	Obed	_____
Elkanah	Hannah	Samuel	_____
David	Bathsheba	Solomon	_____
Zechariah	Elizabeth	John	_____
Joseph	Mary	Jesus	_____

```
S  U  S  E  J  M  A  R  Y  E  C  Z  G  H  T  D
L  M  I  N  O  A  B  E  L  V  I  O  T  L  Z  A
O  B  D  A  S  D  O  O  B  E  D  U  J  Z  E  D
V  L  A  X  E  A  W  C  A  Q  R  Y  D  O  C  B
E  R  V  T  P  M  E  L  I  Z  A  B  E  T  H  M
T  R  I  S  H  L  M  E  M  A  P  X  C  W  A  N
E  Z  D  F  G  S  O  L  O  M  O  N  A  H  R  X
L  F  U  N  J  H  H  U  M  H  A  R  A  S  I  H
K  J  K  S  A  M  U  E  L  M  N  R  S  T  A  O
A  X  W  N  C  E  L  T  B  F  B  G  I  K  H  M
N  B  N  P  O  B  E  N  J  A  M  I  N  C  N  E
A  A  E  S  B  O  T  D  A  U  G  H  T  E  R  W
H  L  E  H  C  A  R  Z  J  O  Y  O  N  O  S  O
```

(dad, daughter, fun, home, joy, love, mom, son)

PRAYER

Our Father who is in Heaven,
You made me and I am Your child.
Thanks for loving me and forgiving me and caring about me.
Help me remember when You discipline me that it's for my own good
and because You love me, not because You're mad at me.
I'm so glad I belong to Your big family.
I'm so glad I can call You my Father.
In Jesus' name, amen.

G

· · · · · · · · · · · · · ·

GOD IS GRACIOUS

The LORD is gracious and compassionate, slow to anger and rich in love. The LORD is good to all; he has compassion on all he has made.

Psalm 145:8-9

EVERYONE NEEDS KINDNESS

Moving is the pits! thought Josh. *Why can't my dad have a normal job like other dads?*

Josh hated new towns and new schools. Sitting alone in the lunchroom, he opened his brown bag and pulled out a sandwich.

At a nearby table, kids were telling jokes and laughing. At another table everyone was talking at the same time about yesterday's soccer game. *It's rough losing old friends,* Josh thought. *And it's tough making new ones.*

"Hi, there! Mind if I eat lunch with you?" A tall kid with a crooked smile sat down across from Josh. "You're new here, aren't you?"

Josh swallowed a mouthful of dry bread and tuna. "Yeah. Moved in last week. I'm Josh—Josh Wilkins."

"My name's Brian. Do you play soccer, Josh?" he asked. "There's a game after lunch. Sure could use you on our team."

□   □   □

Discussion

1. Have you ever moved?

2. If so, have you ever felt like Josh did?

3. Why is a little bit of kindness so important?

Understanding words

Gracious and *compassionate* have a lot in common. We could say they both belong to the *kindness* family.

Kind means doing something good or showing real concern for someone.

Gracious means being thoughtful, *kind*, helpful, and caring.

Compassionate means feeling so sorry for people who are unhappy or hurting that you do something *kind* for them.

Talking about kindness

1. Who are the people you know who are kind, gracious, or compassionate?

2. What have they done that makes you think so?

DISCOVERING THAT GOD IS GRACIOUS

1. Unscramble the words below and you will find evidence of God's great kindness. If you have trouble, the Scriptures will help. Don't forget to color-code them.

a. Psalm 10:14

E	S	E		B	O	R	U	L	E	T		N	A	D		F	I	G	E	R

P	H	E	R	L	E		F	O		H	E	T		T	H	E	S	A	F	R	E	L	S

b. 2 Kings 13:23

D	E	H	O	W	S		R	O	C	N	N	E	C

c. Nehemiah 9:17

A		V	I	G	R	O	N	F	I	G		O	G	D

W	O	S	L		O	T		G	E	N	R	A

G	I	B	A	N	D	O	U	N		N	I		V	O	L	E

I	D	D		T	O	N		S	E	T	R	E	D		M	E	T	H

d. Psalm 111:4-5

D	E	P	O	R	V	I	S		D	O	F	O

S	R	E	M	M	E	B	E	R		S	H	I		T	A	N	V	O	N	C	E

Two promises to remember
(Use purple, brown, and yellow to color-code.)

2. Isaiah 30:19 says, "How _____ he [God] will be when you _____ for _____! As soon as he _____, he will _____ you."

3. Lamentations 3:22-23 gives us encouragement: "Because of the LORD's great _____ we are not consumed, for his _____ never _____. They are new every _____; great is your _____."

A word picture of a gracious God

The word *kindness* is your only clue in this "linking word puzzle."
To solve this puzzle, follow these directions:

1. Read aloud Isaiah 30:18 and Isaiah 40:11 (*New International Version* needed).
2. Assign someone to announce what kind of word is needed in the puzzle and to fill in the empty squares. Example: "The first word has five letters, with a 'K' as the last letter."
3. The rest of the family searches the two verses for the word. Whoever finds it says it aloud, and spells it if necessary.
4. Continue linking words until the puzzle is completed.

CHALLENGE

Many stories in the Old Testament reveal how good God is to people who love Him and ask for His help. Watch for God's kindness in this play based on the story of baby Samuel and his mother, Hannah, from 1 Samuel 1:1-2:21.

Our tenderhearted God

Narrator—storyteller who describes action between scenes
Elkanah—religious man of Ramah who had two wives
Hannah—first wife, tenderhearted and godly
Peninnah—second wife, a jealous troublemaker
Child—youngest child of Peninnah and Elkanah
Eli—the priest at the Tabernacle in Shiloh

Scene 1—On the road to Shiloh

Narrator: Every year Elkanah takes his family on a fifteen-mile journey to Shiloh where they worship God in the Tabernacle and celebrate the harvest. Elkanah leads his donkey, loaded with their supplies. His two wives follow behind, while Peninnah's children play games along the way.

Peninnah: (bragging) What joy my children bring me! I'm truly blessed of God. (teasing) And you, poor Hannah, why don't you have any children?

Hannah: I want children very much. I don't know why God has not allowed me to be a mother.

Peninnah: (hatefully) It's a curse and you know it. You must have done something very wicked. That's why you can't give Elkanah a son.

Hannah: That's not fair, Peninnah. I respect and obey my husband. I love and worship the Lord God.

Peninnah: (sneering) You must be hiding some dreadful sin. It's your fault that Elkanah married me. He needed a second wife to give him sons to carry on his name. Oh, I know he loves you more than he loves me, but. . . .

Hannah: (interrupting, in tears) Stop it, Peninnah. I suffer enough without you tormenting me all the time.

Peninnah: Look at my children playing around their father. See how happy they make Elkanah? My children will inherit all his property. Someday I'll be a grandmother. And you? Someday you'll be forgotten.

Scene 2—Shiloh, campground around the Tabernacle

Narrator: All day long people from Israel arrive for the Feast of Booths. For eight days, the Jews will celebrate the fall harvest of olives, grapes, and grain.

Elkanah: Children, go get some branches so we can build our booth.

Child: What's the booth for, Father?

Elkanah: We need a place to live while we celebrate and thank God for the good harvest He has given us. Besides, living in these little huts reminds us of the forty years our ancestors wandered in the wilderness before they settled in this wonderful land.

Peninnah: It's a happy time, my child. There will be music and dancing, games and contests.

Elkanah: But it's more than that, Peninnah. You have forgotten the important part. Every day we'll worship at the Tabernacle. Every day we'll offer sacrifices to God.

Peninnah: (ignoring Elkanah) And best of all, your father gives us presents.

Elkanah: (sigh) Peninnah, help the children gather branches. I'm going to find Hannah.

Peninnah: She's sitting under that huge oak tree. She won't eat the lunch I prepared. I think she's sick.

Scene 3—Behind the oak tree

Elkanah: Hannah, your eyes are red. Why have you been crying?

Hannah: Oh, Elkanah, I want to be a mother. I want a baby. My heart aches because I have no son.

Elkanah: I love you very much, Hannah. You're more important to me than ten sons. Isn't my love enough to make you happy? Come along now and help us build the booth.

Narrator: By evening, the campground was filled with booths and tents of all shapes and sizes. Every morning the people worshiped God in the Tabernacle. Every evening they sang and danced. For six days Hannah ate nothing. She looked thin and sad. On the seventh day, she went to the Tabernacle alone and knelt before the altar.

Scene 4—In the Tabernacle

Hannah: (crying and praying softly) O Lord Almighty, You know everything. You know how sad I am. You know how badly I want a son. I love You, O God, and I try hard to keep Your commandments. Hear my prayer. Please give me a son, and I promise I will give him back to You to serve You in Your Temple.

Eli: (tapping Hannah on the shoulder) I've been watching you from behind the pillars. Your mouth is moving but I hear no sounds. Are you drunk? (scolding) You shouldn't come before God in this condition.

Hannah: Oh, no, sir. I'm not a wicked woman. But I'm very sad. I've been telling God about my problem. I asked for something special, and I made a sacred promise.

Eli: I'm glad you're not drunk. You seem sincere. Go in peace. May God give you what you have asked of Him.

Hannah: Thank you for your blessing. I think God really cares about my problem. And I believe He heard me and will answer my prayer.

Narrator: When Hannah returned to the booth, she was smiling. She ate a hearty dinner with the family. The next day, they tore down the booth, packed up their belongings, and went home. A year later Hannah had a baby boy, and she named him Samuel. Hannah nursed her son and took good care of him. As he grew, she told him about God. She taught him to obey the Holy Scriptures. Hannah loved Samuel very much. But she did not forget her promise to God. When the time came, Hannah packed Samuel's clothes and took him to Shiloh.

Scene 5—The Tabernacle in Shiloh

Hannah: Sir, do you remember me?

Eli: It's been a few years, but I remember. You were sad and deeply troubled. Did God answer your prayer?

Hannah: Yes. God was gracious to me. I asked God to give me a son, and I promised I would give him back to the Lord for as long as he lives. Sir, this is Samuel, my gift *from* God and my gift *to* God.

Eli: Well, well! He's just a little lad, but he can learn to be the Lord's helper. He'll live here in the Tabernacle with me, and I'll take good care of him.

Elkanah: My son, we'll pray for you every day, and we'll visit you when we come to worship in the Tabernacle.

Hannah: And, Samuel, I'll bring you new clothes every year.

Eli: Let's pray together before you go home.

Elkanah: Thank You, Lord, for my son Samuel. We are going to miss him. Please protect him and help him grow up to be loving and kind.

Hannah: Dear God, I'm so happy. You have answered my prayer and solved my problem. You are so kind and good.

Eli: O God, these parents are showing their love for You by giving their only son to serve You. Bless them and give them many sons and daughters to take the place of Samuel. Amen.

Narrator: As young Samuel grew older and bigger, he became God's special helper. Everyone liked him, and God was pleased with everything he did. God did not forget Hannah and Elkanah. His kindness was more than they expected. God blessed them and gave them three more sons and two daughters.

□   □   □

Discussion

1. How did God show His compassion to Hannah?

2. Why do you think God was kind to Hannah? (See Lamentations 3:25.)

☆ APPLICATION

1. a. Has anyone ever treated you the way that Peninnah treated Hannah?

   b. How did you feel?

   c. What did you do?

2. What three things should you do next time someone is unkind to you? You'll find some suggestions in Isaiah 30:19 and Ephesians 4:32.

   a. _____

   b. _____

   c. _____

G⁷¹

PRAYER

Write your own prayer, thanking God for His kindness to your family. Tell Him about any problems you are now facing. Ask for His help as Hannah did.

You can close with this benediction, adapted from Numbers 6:24-25.

Lord, bless us and keep us.
Smile down upon us and be gracious to us.
Watch over us and give us Your peace.
Amen.

GOD IS HOLY

Your ways, O God, are holy.

Psalm 77:13

ONE HUNDRED PERCENT PURE AND PERFECT

Amy was helping her mother with the grocery shopping. Because of her new interest in health foods, Amy read the labels of everything her mother put into the shopping cart.

At the juice shelf, Amy picked up a bottle of orange juice. She read, "Filtered water, high fructose corn syrup, orange juice concentrate, natural flavors, fumaric acid, vitamin C."

"*Yu-uck!*" she said, shoving it back on the shelf. She picked up another. It simply read, "One hundred percent pure orange juice from Florida."

"That's the one I want," said Amy, putting the bottle into the shopping cart.

□   □   □

Discussion

1. a. What was the difference between the two bottles of juice?

   b. What's the difference between a polluted river and a fresh mountain stream?

   c. Between polluted air and clean air?

2. What does *pure* mean? (Check the right answers; correct the wrong one.)

   a. ___ Not mixed with anything else.

   b. ___ Not polluted.

   c. ___ Separated from almost all contamination.

God is pure.

Let's study some verses showing that God is pure, that He is totally separated from everything that's bad or sinful.

3. First John 1:5 says, "God is _____; in him there is no

   _____ at all."

4. David sang of God: "The LORD is _____; he is my Rock,

   and there is no _____ in him" (Psalm 92:15).

5. In Habakkuk 1:13 we read this description of God: "Your eyes are too _____ to look on _____; you cannot tolerate _____."

Discussion

1. What would you call it, if you scored one hundred percent correct on a math test? Or hit the bull's-eye in a dart game? Or sunk the basketball through the hoop ten times in a row?

2. Have you ever wished you were perfect? If you could change something about yourself, what would it be?

3. What does *perfect* mean? (Check the right answers; correct the wrong one.)

    a. ____ Supremely excellent.

    b. ____ Making only one mistake.

    c. ____ Having no faults, no blemishes.

God is perfect.

Let's study some verses showing that God is perfect—that everything He thinks and says and does is right.

4. In 2 Samuel 22:31 we are told, "As for God, his way is _____; the word of the LORD is _____."

5. Moses recited these words: "Oh, praise the greatness of our God! He is the Rock, his works are _____, and all his ways are _____. A faithful God who does no _____, _____ and _____ is he" (Deuteronomy 32:3-4).

6. James mentions God's perfection: "When tempted, no one should say, 'God is tempting me.' For God cannot be _____ by _____, nor does he tempt anyone" (James 1:13).

UNDERSTANDING GOD'S HOLINESS

The house was filled with the tempting aroma of cookies baking. Brett tossed his jacket on a chair and reached for a warm chocolate-chip cookie.

Mother called from upstairs, "Don't touch the cookies on the blue plate. They're *set aside* for company. Help yourself to the cookies on the tray."

Discussion

1. What do you think was different about the cookies on the blue plate from those on the tray?

2. a. What item of clothing do you have set aside for special occasions?

   b. Why is it special?

God is set apart.

God is set apart from His creation. His character, words, and works are high above all beings.

3. In praying to God, Hannah recognized that "There is no one _____ like the LORD; there is _____ besides you; there is no Rock like our God" (1 Samuel 2:2).

4. God's supremacy is declared in Isaiah 55:8-9: "For my _____ are not your thoughts, neither are your _____ my ways," declares the LORD. "As the heavens are _____ than the earth, so are my _____ higher than your ways and my _____ than your thoughts."

5. In Psalm 5:4, David wrote, "You are not a God who takes pleasure in _____; with you the _____ cannot dwell."

Holiness is God's greatest attribute.

Nothing can be compared to God's holiness. The Scriptures refer to this attribute more than any other, and it is the only one emphasized through repetition. Copy these verses.

Isaiah 6:3 _____

_____

Revelation 4:8 _____

_____

☆ APPLICATION

1. Read Psalm 30:4 and Revelation 15:4. List three ways we should respond to our Holy God.

   a. _____

   b. _____

   c. _____

2. Talk together about these questions. A dictionary will help.
   a. What does it mean to *fear* the Lord? (Hint: It doesn't mean to be scared of God.)

   b. How can your family bring *glory* to His name?

   c. How can you *praise* God?

CHALLENGE

Complete these sentences with something you understand about God.

Because God is pure, _____ .

Because God is perfect, _____ .

Because God is set apart, _____ .

Because God is holy, I _____ .

PRAYER

O God,
You alone are holy.
There is no one in Heaven or earth like You.
Your ways are higher and holier than our ways,
and Your thoughts are deeper than our thoughts.
Thank You for Your Son, Jesus, who died on the cross
to take away our sins so we can fellowship with You.
Lord, I invite You to sit on the throne of my heart
and to be in control of my life.
I want to belong to You.
I want to obey You and serve You.
In Jesus' name, amen.

GOD IS INCOMPARABLE

"To whom will you compare me?
Or who is my equal?" says the
Holy One.

Isaiah 40:25

WORSHIPING OTHER GODS

When God created man, He put within man the desire to worship God, the Creator. This desire is so strong that when man does not know the true God, he will make or invent a god to worship.

These other gods may be things in nature like the sun, moon, rocks, or trees. While living in South Korea for four years, I saw a tree that people worshiped because they believed a spirit lived in it. To please this spirit, people had tied hundreds of colored ribbons and narrow pieces of cloth to its branches.

Other gods may be idols carved out of wood or molded from silver or gold. They often represent people (real and imaginary) or nature or animals. Remember how the Israelites made the golden calf and were worshiping it when Moses came down from the mountain with the Ten Commandments?

SEARCHING FOR THE TRUTH

The question: The Lord asks, "To whom will you compare me or count me equal? To whom will you liken me that we may be compared?" (Isaiah 46:5).

The answer: The Lord God is greater than . . .

_____ Psalm 89:6-7

_____ Psalm 135:5

_____ Jeremiah 10:6-7

_____ Habakkuk 2:18-20

_____ James 2:19

God answers His own question. Copy Isaiah 46:9 below.

_____

_____

_____

_____

UNDERSTANDING WORDS

Have you ever pretended to be a doctor? Let's be word surgeons and operate on the word *incomparable* (in kom' per a bul). We'll cut it into four parts and see what each means.

> in-com-par-able
> 2 prefixes: in = not; com = with
> 1 root: par = equal
> 1 suffix: able = able to be

Putting it back together, the word means: not able to be equal with. Nothing—neither man, nor angels, nor idols, nor gods, nor the devil—is equal with the Lord God.

Our God is incomparable. He is unequaled, unsurpassed.

PROVING THAT GOD IS INCOMPARABLE

What makes idols different from God?

1. Read the following verses and fill in the missing letters.

a. Psalm 135:15-17—Idols are made by __ __ __ **D** __ of __ __ **N**. Idols cannot __ **P** __ __ __ , nor __ **E** __ , nor __ __ **R** .

b. Isaiah 46:6-7—Idols cannot **M** __ __ __ . They do not __ __ __ **W** __ __ . They cannot __ __ **V** __ man from his __ **R** __ __ __ __ **L** __ __ .

Idols are as powerless as a scarecrow in a cornfield.

What makes the Lord God different from other gods?

2. Read the following verses and fill in the missing letters. (Don't forget to color-code these verses.)

a. Exodus 18:10-11—God __ __ __ **C** __ __ **D** the __ __ __ __ **P** __ __ .

b. Deuteronomy 3:24—God does __ __ __ **D** __ and mighty __ __ __ **K** __ .

c. 1 Samuel 2:2—God is __ __ __ Y .

d. 2 Chronicles 6:14—God K __ __ __ __ His covenant of
__ __ V __ .

e. Isaiah 43:10-11—God is our only __ __ V __ R .

CHALLENGE

The time machine will take you back to Old Testament days again. Television reporter Chris Kelly and the camera crew from BBS (Bible Broadcasting System) are going to cover the Olympic contest between the gods held on Mount Carmel, about 865 BC. Elijah, God's champion, will challenge the prophets of Baal.

Olympic contest between the gods
1 Kings 16:29-18:39

Chris Kelly—BBS reporter
Elijah—a bold and rugged prophet of God
Obadiah—a servant of God in King Ahab's palace
King Ahab—the most wicked king of Israel
Zimdar—a prophet of Baal, the sky god

Scene 1—On top of Mount Carmel

Chris: I'm Chris Kelly, reporting to you from Carmel mountain in Israel. Thousands of people have gathered for this Olympic contest between the gods. Coming toward me is a muscular man with long hair. He's wearing sandals and a leather garment. A shaggy shawl is thrown over one shoulder. Let's speak to him. Good morning, Elijah. I hear you arranged this contest. Please explain what is going to happen.

Elijah: The Israelites have forgotten Jehovah. They worship the heathen god Baal. Today, we will prove to the people that Baal can do nothing and that Jehovah is the true God.

Chris: How do you plan to do that?

Elijah: You'll have to wait and watch like everyone else. Now I must make an announcement. (loudly) People of Israel, how long will you bounce back and forth between two religions? One day you bow to Baal. The next day you pray to God. You cannot serve both. If the Lord is God, follow Him; but if Baal is God, follow him.

Chris: (facing camera) The crowd is quiet. Elijah is a forceful man.

Elijah: Today, 450 prophets of Baal are here. And I, the only prophet of the Lord God, challenge them. Here are my instructions. Get two bulls: one for them, one for me. Let the prophets of Baal cut their bull into pieces and put it on the wood, but they must not set fire to it. I will prepare the other bull and put it on the wood, but I will not set fire to it either. Then you pray to Baal, and I will pray to Jehovah. Whoever answers by fire—He is God.

People: What you say is good. We will do it.

Chris: (facing camera) While men are bringing the bulls and chopping down oak trees for the altars, let's interview some of the people here on Carmel mountain. This man beside me is Obadiah, a believer in Jehovah. I hear that he's an intelligent, capable man, and that he is in charge of the king's palace.

Obadiah, we know Jehovah is the deliverer of the Israelites. But who is Baal?

Obadiah: Baal is the chief god of the Phoenicians. He's considered to be the god of the sky, in charge of the sun and rains. People believe he has power to increase the crops, the flocks, and the children of farm families.

Chris: Why do the Israelites worship the Phoenician god?

Obadiah: It's a sad story. Phoenicia is a country northwest of Israel, along the coast. In order to keep peace, the two countries signed a treaty. To make sure the agreement would never be broken, King Ahab married Jezebel, the daughter of the king of Phoenicia.

Chris: I'm beginning to see the picture. Jezebel worships Baal, the Phoenician god.

Obadiah: Yes, but more than that. Jezebel is a fanatic. She wanted the Israelites to bow down to Baal, so she demanded that King Ahab build temples throughout Israel. Then she brought to the palace hundreds of Baal's prophets. They live on the palace grounds and eat at Queen Jezebel's table.

Chris: I heard Elijah say he's the only prophet of God left. What happened to the rest?

Obadiah: Jezebel hates the prophets of Jehovah. She has put many to death. Others are hiding.

Chris: Elijah must be a bold man to demand this contest.

Obadiah: You're right. Elijah has been called Jehovah's champion. Jezebel would like to see him killed.

Chris: Let's listen now. Elijah is shouting something.

Elijah: Who will speak for the prophets of Baal?

Zimdar: I'm Zimdar, the head prophet. What shall we do?

Elijah: You be first, since there are so many of you. Choose one of the bulls. Prepare it for the offering. Call to your god Baal, but do *not* light the fire.

Zimdar: (angrily) This challenge shall not go unanswered. Baal will certainly hear our cry.

Chris: (facing camera) This is an amazing sight. Hundreds of prophets of Baal have surrounded the altar. Now they're kneeling and praying loudly.

Zimdar: O Baal, we worship you. Send fire down upon our offering. Hear our prayer and answer us.

Chris: (facing camera) Nothing is happening. The prophets are shouting louder. Now they're standing. With hands waving wildly in the air, the prophets are dancing around the altar. Nothing is happening. This may take a while. I see King Ahab sitting in his royal chariot. Perhaps he'll answer some questions. King Ahab, how did this contest come about?

Ahab: It's all because of that troublemaker, Elijah.

Chris: What do you mean?

Ahab: Three and a half years ago, Elijah marched into my palace in Samaria. He said God had sent him. He said that because the people were wicked, no rain or dew would fall until he prayed for it.

Chris: And did that really happen?

Ahab: Oh, yes. There has been no rain for over three years. The rivers have dried up. The wheat won't grow. The cattle are dying.

Chris: Sounds serious. Did you send for Elijah?

Ahab: No. He came to me. He accused me of causing the problem. He said it was because I disobeyed the Lord and followed Baal.

Chris: He actually spoke that way to the king of Israel?

Ahab: That's not all. He demanded I call together the prophets of Baal and the people of Israel to meet him on this mountain. So here we are.

Chris: Thank you, King Ahab, for speaking with us. (turning to the camera) It's noon here on Mount Carmel. Baal's prophets are still begging for fire to fall.

Elijah: (mockingly) Prophets of Baal, shout louder! Surely Baal is a living god. He must be busy. Perhaps he's thinking. Maybe he's sleeping or traveling. Shout louder so he can hear you!

Scene 2—Four hours later

Chris: Folks, we've been waiting all afternoon. Here's Obadiah to tell us what's been happening.

Obadiah: The prophets of Baal have been dancing and shouting all day. Now they are cutting themselves with knives and swords. Many of them are bleeding, but that's all part of their worship ceremony.

Chris: In spite of all this, Baal does nothing?

Obadiah: Because he is not God. There is only one God.

Chris: Oh, look! Elijah is digging a ditch about three feet wide around the stone altar he just built.

Obadiah: Men are bringing the bull to Elijah. He'll cut it into pieces and lay it on the wood as an offering to God. Now he's giving instructions to four men.

Elijah: Young men, fill four barrels with water and pour the water over the bull and the wood.

Chris: (surprised) They're soaking everything! The offering will never burn if it's wet.

Elijah: Young men, do it again. (pause) Do it a third time.

Obadiah: Now the meat, the wood, and the ground have been soaked three times, and the ditch is full of water.

Chris: The restless crowd is quiet, intently watching. There's a gentle breeze blowing across the mountaintop as Elijah stretches his hands toward Heaven.

Elijah: O Holy One of Israel, You alone are God. Send fire upon this offering. Hear and answer my prayer, O Lord. Then these people will know You love them and want them to return to You.

Chris: (with excitement) Fire is falling from the sky! The wood is burning! The bull is burning! Like a thirsty dog, flames are lapping up the water in the ditch and even the stones of the altar and the dirt. The prophets of Baal are running away. The Israelites are kneeling to pray.

People: Jehovah is God! The LORD—He is God!

Chris: Ladies and gentlemen of my television audience, we have seen a mighty miracle. I must agree with Elijah, Obadiah, and the people of Israel. The LORD is God. No other god can be compared to the Holy God of the Israelites. And now, from your television crew at BBS and from Mount Carmel, goodbye and thanks for joining us.

□   □   □

Discussion

1. Why were King Ahab and Queen Jezebel considered the most wicked rulers Israel ever had?

2. How did God prove that He was greater than Baal?

APPLICATION

1. Do you know anyone who worships other gods or idols? If something becomes more important to a person than obeying and worshiping the Lord God, then that may become a god to him.

2. Talk about how things can become gods if we are not careful. Each family member will have different ideas depending upon his or her age. Discuss these subjects:

   • money
   • popularity (being liked, having lots of friends)
   • power or position (being a leader)
   • possessions or hobbies
   • success (in sports, career)

PRAYER

Let volunteers say sentence prayers, expressing praise and thanksgiving, or making a confession or request that has been prompted by this application. Close by reading together Psalm 86:8,10.

"Among the gods there is none like you, O Lord;
no deeds can compare with yours.
For you are great and do marvelous deeds;
you alone are God."

J

GOD IS A JUST JUDGE

Let them sing before the LORD, for
he comes to judge the earth. He will
judge the world in righteousness
and the peoples with equity.

Psalm 98:9

FAVORITISM OR JUSTICE?

Scott stood before the judge, waiting for the decision. It's true he'd been driving his sports car too fast. And, yes, he'd been drinking just a little. But he wasn't worried. He knew things would work out okay.

"Young man," said the judge. "You have broken the law. Two laws, in fact. Speeding in a school zone is a serious offense. And drinking while driving is even worse. You could have killed someone, you know."

"Yes, your Honor," Scott said politely with a smile.

The judge pounded his gavel on the court bench. "Young man, here is my verdict. You may not drive a car for six months. Give your driver's license to the bailiff."

Scott's smile disappeared. "Hey, Dad, I'm your son, remember?"

The judge came from behind the bench and put his arm around his son. "Scott, at home I'm your father and offer you love. In the court, I'm your judge and I offer you justice."

Tears filled Scott's eyes. "But I'm your own flesh and blood," he stammered. "Doesn't that count for something?"

"You've broken the law and must be punished. I can't treat you differently from another teenager who broke the law last week. When I wear this black robe, I'm a judge, and I must be fair and just to everyone."

□   □   □

Discussion

1. How is God like the judge in this story?

2. How are some people like Scott in their attitude toward God?

3. How would you explain the words *justice* and *equity*?

God deals fairly.

Being fair means showing no favoritism. It means treating everyone as equal, regardless of personal feelings.

4. Fill in the blanks with the words that describe fairness.

   a. Deuteronomy 10:17 gives us insight regarding God's fairness: "For the LORD your God is God of gods and Lord of lords, the great God, mighty and awesome, who shows no

   _____ and accepts _____."

   b. We read in 2 Chronicles 19:7, "For with the LORD our God

   there is no _____ or _____ or

   _____."

   c. In Psalm 96:10 David writes, "Say among the nations, 'The

   LORD reigns.' . . . He will _____ the peoples with

   _____."

   d. In Acts 10:34-35 we are told, "Then Peter began to speak: 'I now realize how true it is that God does not show

   _____ but _____ men from _____ nation who fear him and do what is right.'"

   e. God's fairness is clearly stressed in Romans 2:9-11: "There will

   be trouble and distress for _____ human being who

   does evil: first for the _____, then for the

   _____; but glory, honor and peace for _____

   who does good. . . . For God does not show _____."

God deals righteously.

5. The definition of *righteous* is easy to remember. It means doing what is *right*. The words *righteous* or *righteousness* appear in the Scriptures listed below, but there are also other words that help explain righteousness. Can you match the Scriptures with the synonyms?

	SYNONYMS
Psalm 9:8	Truth
Psalm 33:4-5	Right, trustworthy
Psalm 75:2	Uprightly
Psalm 96:13	Justice
Psalm 119:137-138	Right, true, just

☆APPLICATION

1. a. When have you been treated unfairly or perhaps been blamed or punished for something you didn't do? Talk about it.

   b. How did you feel?

2. Human beings don't always make right judgments, but God does.
   a. What does it mean to you that God is a just Judge—fair, impartial, and righteous in all He does?

   b. How will knowing this cause you to change any of your attitudes or actions?

Tic-tac-toe code

To find out what God's justice is compared to, exchange the tic-tac-toe symbols for the letters they represent.

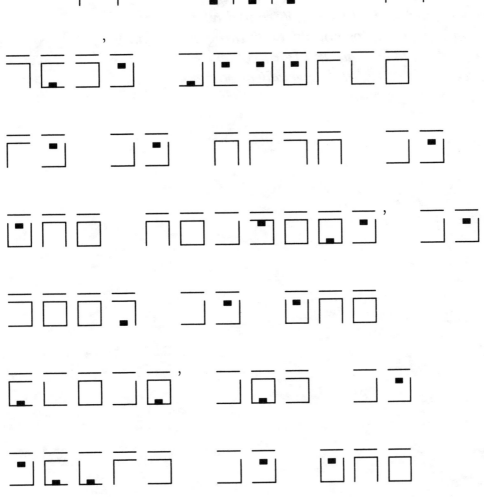

PRAYER

O Lord,
You are a righteous God.
Everything You do is right and just.
The Bible says You're fair in dealing with people.
And I believe that, even though
sometimes it seems like I always get punished,
and other kids, who do worse things than I do, get away with it.
Help me to live the way that pleases You,
and to remember that You are the Judge
who will judge all of us equally someday.
Forgive me, Lord, for not always treating people fairly.
Remind me to be kind and fair to others
at school, in sports, and especially at home.
In Jesus' name, amen.

K

GOD IS OUR KING

How awesome is the LORD Most
High, the great King over all the
earth!

Psalm 47:2

FAMOUS KINGS

Beginning with nursery rhymes and continuing throughout history, you have read about many kings. How many famous kings can you remember? If you need help, choose from the list below.

ACHIEVEMENT	KING
1. Called for his fife, drum, and three fiddlers.	_____
2. Everything he touched turned to gold.	_____
3. His knights sat at the Round Table.	_____
4. First king of Israel, chosen by God.	_____
5. The name of eight kings of England.	_____
6. Wicked king who killed two-year-old boys.	_____
7. The most wicked king of Israel.	_____
8. A musician and a writer who honored God as King.	_____

Arthur	Cole	Henry	Midas
Ahab	David	Herod	Saul

GOD IS KING OVER ALL

Who does the Bible tell us is the greatest King of all? Let's look up some verses to find out.

Use eight colored pencils to match the Scripture with the right description of God as King.

DESCRIPTION

Psalm 24:10   King above all gods
Psalm 29:10-11   He is the King of glory
Psalm 47:8   The eternal King
Psalm 93:1   He is seated on His holy throne
Psalm 95:3   Enthroned as King forever
Jeremiah 10:7   King of the nations
Jeremiah 10:10   Only Ruler, King of kings
1 Timothy 6:15   The Lord reigns, robed in majesty

Understanding words

Every word has two meanings: the exact meaning found in a dictionary (denotation); the suggested meaning pictured in our minds (connotation).

1. *How would you define a king?*

   A dictionary defines him as a man who rules a territory and its people. He usually inherits his position and rules for life.

2. *How do you picture a king?*

   Talk about the image in your mind. Talk about other words that come to mind when you think about a king.

Much more than a ruler

The word *king* connotes more than a man in control of people. Read 1 Chronicles 29:11-12, King David's prayer of praise to the Lord.

3. Fill in the blanks with words that describe the kingship of God.

   "Yours, O LORD, is the _____ and the _____ and the _____ and the _____ and the _____, for _____ in _____ and _____ is yours. Yours, O LORD, is the _____; you are _____ as _____ over all. _____ and _____ come from you; you are the _____ of all _____. In your hands are _____ and _____ to exalt and _____ strength to all."

☆APPLICATION

The Sunday school teacher asked the fifth-grade class to stand up during the opening prayer. Everyone responded except Michael who slouched lower in his chair. The teacher said, "Michael, please stand." Reluctantly Michael stood. "Thank you," said the teacher. Michael mumbled, "I may be standing up on the outside, but I'm still sitting down on the inside."

☐   ☐   ☐

1. Attitude is what you think or how you feel about something. It affects the way you act. Michael obeyed, but what kind of attitude did he have?

2. Describe a time when you have felt like Michael.

3. To honor and worship God as King requires more than obedience. It also requires the right attitude. If you have a poor attitude toward God, how can you change it?

4. What do you think it means when a person says, "God is King of my life"?

CHALLENGE

Memorizing Scripture: *Method 3—Missing Words*

To make this project fun, you'll need a child's chalkboard, chalk, and an eraser. If you don't have a chalkboard, use a poster or tag board and a black felt-tip marker.

1. Print 1 Chronicles 29:11-13 (or another verse from this chapter).
2. The family or group reads the verse together.
3. A person chooses an important word (noun or verb) from the verse. The leader erases that word and puts a short line on the board to represent the missing word. If the verse is long, you may choose two words at a time. If you are using a posterboard, blot out the word with the felt-tip marker.
4. Read the verse together, saying the missing word.
5. Choose another word (or two). Erase and insert lines.
6. Read the verse together. Can you remember the missing words?
7. Continue the process until the important nouns, verbs, and adjectives have been erased.
8. Let people volunteer to read the verse alone. Someone can follow in the Bible to give kind help when needed.

Hidden royalty words

The list below contains twenty-five words associated with a *king*.
Draw a line around each word in the puzzle. They are spelled vertically, horizontally, diagonally, forwards, and backwards. Use four
colored pencils to circle the words.

castle	honor	power	royalty
control	jewels	prince	ruler
crown	king	princess	servants
famous	kingdom	purple	silver
glory	majesty	queen	splendor
gold	palace	rich	throne
			worship

```
H  C  I  R  Z  P  A  L  A  C  E  T  C  E  P
F  T  P  A  O  B  D  E  C  F  A  O  O  H  R
A  I  J  S  L  O  C  M  R  E  N  S  N  S  I
M  P  O  K  I  N  G  D  O  M  R  U  T  V  N
O  J  W  X  I  L  Z  A  W  B  C  N  R  L  C
U  D  E  R  F  G  V  H  N  I  A  B  O  K  E
S  L  P  W  M  N  O  E  T  V  G  O  L  D  S
X  Y  S  Z  E  G  L  O  R  Y  B  C  A  J  S
W  O  P  H  I  L  M  E  K  N  P  O  W  E  R
O  R  L  S  U  T  S  V  B  I  Y  G  A  C  O
R  H  E  X  T  H  R  O  N  E  U  N  B  D  Y
S  E  N  O  W  I  U  M  V  N  E  I  X  I  A
H  U  D  Z  T  A  L  I  S  E  M  K  H  E  L
I  H  O  N  O  R  E  T  U  N  I  D  O  R  T
P  U  R  P  L  E  R  Q  M  A  J  E  S  T  Y
```

K⁹⁷

PRAYER

O Lord,
You are the great God
and King over all the earth.
I want You to be King over my life.
Help me to have good feelings and thoughts about You.
Help me to obey You without complaining or grumbling.
Help me to worship You like King David did,
showing honor and respect,
love and appreciation.
In Jesus' name, amen.

L

GOD IS LOVE

And so we know and rely on the
love God has for us. God is love.

1 John 4:16

LOVE IS A FEELING

Many people have tried to write about love in stories, poems, and songs. Love is not easy to describe, but it's wonderful to feel.

Five special feelings of love
1. Having kind feelings toward another person.
2. Showing concern for his or her health and safety.
3. Wanting to make him or her happy.
4. Longing to be together.
5. Willing to share what you have.

LOVE IS AN ACTION

Love is an action prompted by a feeling or an attitude. Complete these sentences by adding an action toward a person. Tell which one of the five special feelings above caused the action.

Example: Love is a little boy putting a bandage on a puppy's paw (caused by concern for the puppy's health and safety).

Love is a little boy _____ .

Love is a little girl _____ .

Love is a teenager _____ .

Love is a mother _____ .

Love is a father _____ .

Love is a grandmother _____ .

Love is a grandfather _____ .

Love is a teacher _____ .

Love is God _____ .

DEFINING THE LOVE OF GOD

God's love is far greater than anything we feel or do, because God is love. Let's examine some Scriptures that describe God's love for us.

Using six of your colored pencils, draw a line from each reference to its matching quotation. Draw another line from the quotation to the correct definition. Remember to color-code the verses.

	QUOTATION	DEFINITION
Psalm 103:8	"unfailing love . . . will not be shaken"	continues on forever
Psalm 103:11	"his love endures forever"	unchanging; always the same
Psalm 106:1	"high as the heavens are above the earth"	overflowing
Isaiah 54:10	"demonstrates his own love. . . . While we were still sinners"	never stopping; unceasing
Jeremiah 31:3	"abounding in love"	cannot be earned; unconditional
Romans 5:8	"I have loved you with an everlasting love"	too great to be measured

HOW GOD SHOWS HIS LOVE TO US

1. First John 4:9 says, "This is how God showed his love among us:

   He _____ his _____ and _____ Son

   into the _____ that we might _____ through him."

2. Paul writes in Romans 5:5, "God has poured out his

   _____ into our hearts by the Holy _____,

   whom he has _____ us."

A word picture of a loving God

The word *love* is your only clue in this "linking word puzzle." To solve this puzzle, follow these directions:

1. Read aloud Romans 8:38-39 (*New International Version* needed).
2. Assign someone to announce what kind of word is needed in the puzzle and to fill in the empty squares. Example: "The first word has six letters, with an 'O' as the fourth letter."
3. The rest of the family scans the verses for the word. Whoever finds it, says it aloud, and spells it if necessary.
4. Continue linking words until the puzzle is completed.

CHALLENGE

God's love is the greatest love ever known. Jesus Christ is the greatest gift ever given. Here is a play about the Christmas story, told from the viewpoint of angels in Heaven.

Tears in Heaven

Ariel—a little angel (played by a girl)
Pax—a little angel (played by a boy)
Gabriel—a high ranking angel

Scene 1—In Heaven

Narrator: There was sorrow in Heaven. It all seemed so strange to the little angels that sped hither and yon from one end of Heaven to the other, carrying messages from the Master. Ariel, a very little angel, spoke to her best angel-friend, Pax.

Ariel: (seriously) I actually saw those things they call tears in Gabriel's eyes a short while ago. Something terrible must have happened to have caused them.

Pax: I saw them, too. Somebody told me this was the first time tears had ever been shed in Heaven since the earth was created. (cheerfully) Do you remember when God created the earth and sea and sky and everything in them, and how we shouted for joy?

Ariel: Yes, and that wonderful song the morning stars sang together.

Pax: I'll never forget. It's ringing in my ears now.

Ariel: And in mine, too. (sadly) But I cannot understand those tears I saw in Gabriel's eyes, and the sadness that seems to cloud the faces of all the big angels.

Pax: I'm sure it has something to do with those human beings that were created on earth. The Father loves them very much, and yet I heard they have forgotten Him.

Ariel: Isn't it terrible?

Pax: And do you know, I heard the strangest story. I heard that God the Father is going to send the Lord Jesus down to earth to save the humans.

This play was adapted from "Angels in Tears," a short story in *The Burning Bush*, author unknown.

Narrator: Ariel looked at her angel friend in astonishment. For the first time in the few thousand years she had lived, a tear rolled down her cheek.

Ariel: (shocked) He's going to leave us? Going to leave the wonderful glory of Heaven and all the beautiful and lovely things? Going to leave the purity, the holiness, the love of the Father? Going to leave the ivory palaces, golden streets, and the rainbow throne? Going to leave all of us angels who love Him so much? Going to leave all that for those creatures down there? (crying) Oh, it cannot be true! (shakes head)

Narrator: Tears rolled thick and fast down the cheeks of the little angel. Pax wept, too.

Ariel: But what will the Lord Jesus do down there, dear Pax?

Pax: I don't know. I heard someone say He was to be born.

Ariel: (puzzled) Born! Born! What's that?

Pax: (shrugs his shoulders) I've no idea. It seems to be something that happens to the human beings down there.

Ariel: (surprised) You mean to say that He is going to be like them, and take the same body that they have?

Pax: (nodding head sadly) It sounds like that to me. But I cannot understand it at all.

Ariel: When does this strange thing happen, Pax?

Pax: I think it's what they call "tonight" down there. Any time now, I suppose.

Ariel: Then we better hurry back to the City. Perhaps we can learn more about it there.

Scene 2—The Holy City in Heaven

Narrator: There was a great deal of activity in the Holy City when the two little angels returned. Messengers were hurrying to and fro. There were trumpets blowing, and Heaven was filled with the soft rustle of wings as angels came together. Row upon row, rank upon rank, little angels and chief angels bowed before the great white throne. With a terrible sinking feeling in their hearts, the two little angels saw that the throne was vacant. Their beloved Lord Jesus was gone.

Pax: Ariel, look! Oh, look! He's gone! I told you so! (crying)

Narrator: Suddenly, they heard their names called, and Gabriel ordered them into line. While they wondered, Gabriel held up his hand, and there was silence among the angels in Heaven.

Gabriel: (loudly) You are gathered together to listen to the most wonderful announcement ever made in the eternal ages in which we live. Our beloved Lord Jesus has left us.

Narrator: The voice of the great angel trembled, and sobs burst from the lips of the gathered angels. Again Gabriel held up his hand to quiet them.

Gabriel: God so loved the world that He sent His only begotten Son to earth to be born as a baby. Our Lord Jesus will take upon Himself the form of man, in order to take away the sin of the world.

Narrator: The angels gasped in astonishment.

Gabriel: On earth tonight, in a little town called Bethlehem, the Son of God will become the son of Mary. By the order of the Father, you will accompany me as we bring the good news to the weary world down below. You will sing the song I give you. The time is here. Let us go.

Narrator: Ariel was trembling with excitement. She and Pax were among those chosen to sing the song of glad tidings to the world. The air was filled with thousands and ten thousands of angels. They swept through the heavens, past the planets and the Milky Way. Down! Down they went through the still night air, leaving the stars twinkling in the skies far above them.

Scene 3—The sky above the shepherds

Narrator: At a signal from Gabriel, the angels folded their wings. While suspended in space, they looked beneath them. They could see a few people dressed in shepherd's robes, lying in the open field around a fire, watching their sheep. Suddenly Gabriel became visible to them. With awestruck faces, the shepherds gazed upon him before covering their faces in terror. They listened breathlessly as Gabriel spoke.

Gabriel: Fear not: for, I bring you good tidings of great joy, which shall be to all people. For unto you is born this day in the city of David, a Savior, which is Christ the Lord.

L 105

Narrator: As Gabriel finished the message, all the angels became visible. With the rest of the heavenly messengers, Ariel and Pax lifted their voices and praised God. They could not understand the mystery of it all, but the everlasting and unlimited love of God to the world caused them to lift their voices again and again.

Ariel: Glory to God in the highest Heaven!

Pax: Peace on earth among men of good will.

Narrator: They knew that this was the song to sing, and with all their might they sang it. It floated out upon the still night air. It delighted the shepherds who heard it. The night breeze that blew over the fields of Bethlehem caught it and carried it heavenward, where it echoed around the beautiful throne of God. Again at a signal from Gabriel, the heavenly messengers moved upward.

Ariel: What does it mean, Pax?

Pax: I cannot tell, but it was wonderful, wasn't it? Think of it, going to save them from sin! Oh, Ariel, how glad they must be on earth to have Jesus there! And how eagerly they will receive such a Savior! I hope it will not take long to save them all. It will be so lonely in Heaven without Him.

Narrator: And tears fell from the eyes of the two little angels.

□   □   □

Discussion

1. Why did God send His only Son to earth?

2. One of the qualities of love is the willingness to make sacrifices (give up something) for someone we love.
   a. How did God make a sacrifice for us?

   b. How did Jesus Christ make a sacrifice for us?

☆ APPLICATION

1. Pretend someone has just asked you, "What does Christmas really mean?" What would you tell them?

2. Why do you think people reject God's gift?

3. How can we accept God's love and His gift of Jesus Christ?

PRAYER

Our heavenly Father,
thank You for Your great love
that caused You to send Your only Son, Jesus Christ,
to earth to save us from our sins.
We accept Your gift.
We confess our sins and believe You forgive us.
We need Your help daily so we can obey Your Word.
Please fill our hearts with Your love
so we can love others
and tell them what Christmas really means.
In Jesus' name, amen.

M

· · · · · · · · · · · · ·

GOD IS
MERCIFUL

The Lord our God is merciful and
forgiving, even though we have
rebelled against him; we have not
obeyed the LORD our God or kept
the laws he gave us.

Daniel 9:9

M¹⁰⁹

LUCK OR MERCY?

The car sped down the highway.

Billy was sitting in the back seat, looking out the window. "Daddy, there's a police car with a flashing red light."

"Oh, no!" Mr. Bowers groaned and pulled over to the curb.

The policeman walked up to the window. "Let me see your driver's license. You were going sixty miles an hour in a forty-five-mile zone. What's the hurry?" he asked.

"I'm sorry, officer. We're going to see my daughter in the school play. We just got a late start."

"Mr. Bowers, I should give you a ticket for speeding. You deserve it, and you'd have to pay a fine. But, since your driving record is clean, I'll give you a warning today. Next time start earlier, and watch those speed limits."

"Thanks, officer. I'll remember that," said Mr. Bowers politely, putting his license back into his billfold.

"I call that luck," said Billy.

"I call it mercy," said Mr. Bowers. "I broke the law. Even though I deserved a ticket, the policeman didn't give me one."

□   □   □

Discussion

1. a. What should a person expect when he or she breaks laws or rules?

   b. What rules of your home or school have you broken recently?

   c. What kind of punishment did you receive?

   • No television tonight?
   • Getting grounded for a week?
   • No allowance for a month?

2. What do you call it when a parent or teacher cuts a punishment in half or dismisses the punishment altogether?

Understanding words

Merciful means showing kind and compassionate treatment, especially to someone who has broken a law or rule.

Here are three words that belong to the *mercy* family.

- *Pardon:* To forgive. To release from punishment.
- *Forgive:* To pardon. To give up the wish to punish or get even. To give up all hard feelings toward someone.
- *Lenient:* To be mild or gentle; not strict or stern.

Defining mercy from the Bible

3. Ezra 9:13 reads, "Our God, you have _____ us _____ than our sins have deserved."

4. In Psalm 103:10 David wrote, "He does not _____ us as our sins _____ or _____ us according to our iniquities [sins]."

5. We learn from Psalm 78:38 about God's treatment of the Hebrews in the wilderness: "Yet he was _____; he _____ their iniquities and did not _____ them. Time after time he restrained his _____ and did not stir up his full _____."

GOD'S MERCY LONG AGO

Nehemiah led the Hebrews back to Jerusalem after seventy years of captivity in Babylon. After the people repaired the broken-down walls, they had a meeting. They confessed their sins and praised God for His help.

In a long prayer, Nehemiah reviewed Israel's history. He told how God guided them and forgave their sins continually. Read part of that prayer in Nehemiah 9:16-18.

1. What were seven sins of the people?

_____

_____

_____

2. What six things did Nehemiah praise God for?

_____

_____

_____

Read Nehemiah 9:28,31.

3. When did God have mercy on His people?

_____

4. How did God show His mercy?

_____

GOD'S MERCY TODAY

Below are questions with multiple answers. Read them carefully and circle the best answer. Check the Scriptures to see if you are right.

1. How does God feel about showing mercy? (Micah 7:18)
   a. He's unwilling but must keep His promises.
   b. He's impatient and gets angry when we keep sinning.
   c. He gets tired of hearing the same prayers.
   d. He enjoys showing mercy.

2. What does God do with our sins? (Micah 7:19)
   a. He remembers them forever.
   b. He records them permanently in the Book of Life.
   c. He buries them in the sea.
   d. He keeps reminding us of them.

3. What two things does God promise to do? (Hebrews 8:12)
   a. To love and forgive.
   b. To forgive but never forget.
   c. To forgive and forget.
   d. To punish but forgive.

4. Why does God save people from eternal punishment? (Titus 3:5)
   a. Because we do good deeds.
   b. Because of His great mercy.
   c. Because we pray often.
   d. Because we deserve a reward.

5. What must you do to be saved from punishment? (1 John 1:9)
   a. Go to church regularly.
   b. Pray every morning and night.
   c. Read the Bible daily.
   d. Tell God you're sorry for your sins.

☆ APPLICATION

1. Think about the last time your sister, brother, or friend said something mean to you or broke something of yours.
   a. When he said, "I'm sorry," what did you say?

   b. How did you feel?

2. Forgiveness is more than words. It involves changing your feelings toward that person.
   a. When have you had any hard feelings toward someone?

   b. How have you dealt with those feelings?

Here's a verse to remember:

"Bear with each other and forgive whatever grievances you may have against one another. Forgive as the Lord forgave you." (Colossians 3:13)

CHALLENGE

Create your own "linking word puzzle" for other family members to solve, using the grid on page 114. (See samples in chapters G and L.)

Making the answer grid

Draw a grid like the one below. Print *merciful* across the middle.
With pencil, fill in boxes using words from this chapter. (For
example: forgive, forget, love, pardon, God, sins, kind, law, rule,
Jesus, sorry, confess, punish, deserve.)

Making the puzzle grid

Place a clean sheet of paper over your answer grid. Trace only the
boxes that have letters in them. Print *merciful* in the proper boxes.
On the side of the puzzle, list the words you used.

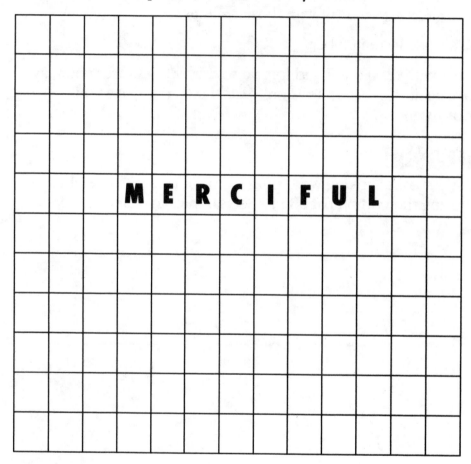

PRAYER

O God,
how merciful You are.
Even when people deserve to be punished,
You are forgiving.
Thank You for sending Jesus
who died on the cross for my sins.
I'm so glad You forgive and forget my sins.
Teach me how to have a forgiving attitude
when other people do wrong to me.
In Jesus' name, amen.

N

. . . .

GOD IS NEAR

One God and Father of all, who is
over all and through all and in all.

Ephesians 4:6

THE UNIVERSAL QUESTION

"Where are you?"

People ask this question at work, at home, at play; in every family, in every country, every day. Here are some examples:

Tim opened the kitchen door and tossed his backpack on the floor. "Where are you, Mom?"

"I'm down here in the laundry room," his mother called back.

□   □   □

The lawyer questioned the man, "Where were you on the night of the murder?"

"At the gym on Fifth Avenue, working out."

□   □   □

"Where have you been with my car?" Dad shouted.

"In a traffic jam on Interstate-forty." Michelle dropped the keys in her father's lap and hurried to her room.

□   □   □

Mother in the laundry room, the man in the gym, and Michelle on Interstate-forty. Each person was in a specific place at a specific time. That's normal for human beings. Don't you agree?

Where are You, God?

1. The scrambled words answer the question, "Where is God?" After you unscramble the words, transfer the numbered letters to the boxes below for the grand answer.

a. "My Presence will go (T H I W) ☐ ☐[4] ☐ ☐ you" (Exodus 33:14).

b. "I will walk (G A N O M) ☐ ☐ ☐ ☐ ☐[1] you and be your God" (Leviticus 26:12).

c. "God will be with you (V E R R H E W E) ☐ ☐ ☐[15] ☐ ☐ ☐[7] ☐ ☐ you go" (Joshua 1:9).

d. "He is at my (T H I R G) ☐[14] ☐ ☐ ☐ ☐ (D A N H) ☐ ☐ ☐ ☐[3] " (Psalm 16:8).

e. "The LORD is (S C O L E) ☐ ☐ ☐ ☐[5] ☐ to the brokenhearted" (Psalm 34:18).

f. "You are (A N E R) ☐ ☐[8] ☐ ☐ , O LORD" . (Psalm 119:151).

g. "God ... is (T O N) ☐ ☐[2] ☐ (F R A) ☐ ☐ ☐[9] from each one of us" (Acts 17:27).

h. "Am I only a God (B R E A N Y) ☐ ☐[13] ☐ ☐ ☐ ☐[10] , ... and not a God (A R F) ☐ ☐ ☐ (W A A Y) ☐ ☐[11] ☐ ☐ ? ... Do not I fill (A H E N V E) ☐ ☐[6] ☐ ☐ ☐ ☐ and (T A R H E) ☐ ☐ ☐ ☐ ☐[12] ?" (Jeremiah 23:23-24).

Grand answer

☐[1] ☐[2] ☐[3]   ☐[4] ☐[5]

☐[6] ☐[7] ☐[8] ☐[9] ☐[10] ☐[11] ☐[12] ☐[13] ☐[14] ☐[15] .

Understanding words

If God fills the Heaven and the earth, He fills all space. If God fills all space, He is all around you. If God is all around you, He is as close as the air you breathe. God is always present; God is everywhere.

Have you heard preachers say, "God is omnipresent"? *Omnipresent* (ahm neh prez' ent) means: God exists everywhere at the same time.

During every minute of every day, God is near you. He is also near people from New York to California, from Brazil to Paris to Tokyo.

2. How can this be? You'll find the answer in John 4:24.

_____

Is there some place God cannot go?

3. Read Psalm 139:7-10 and fill in the blanks.
   "Where can I go from your Spirit?
   Where can I flee from your presence?

   If I go up to the _____, you are there;

   if I make my bed in the _____, you are there.

   If I rise on the wings of the _____,

   if I settle on the _____ side of the _____,
   even there your hand will guide me,

   your right hand will _____ me fast."

Where does God live?

4. a. Acts 17:24 _____

   b. Isaiah 57:15 _____ but also _____

   c. 1 Corinthians 3:16 _____

☆ APPLICATION

1. Parents teach children values. They train them to do what is right; but parents cannot be with their children all the time. How can knowing *God is always near you and living within you* help you each day—in facing temptations and problems?

2. Memorize God's promise in Hebrews 13:5: "Never will I leave you; never will I forsake you."

God is n +

Many stories in the Old Testament prove that God is near. Two of the best ones are about the wise man Daniel who was thrown into the lion's den, and about his three Hebrew friends who were thrown into the fiery furnace. (See Daniel 1:6-7.)

In this rebus puzzle, the pictures, letters, numbers, or combinations of them are substituted for syllables or words. Spelling is not important, but sounds are. Identify the pictures. Follow the add or subtract signs to figure out these names.

An example: + (eye + sack) = ISAAC

1. **A** + + + =

2. **D** + **–C** + =

3. + =

4. + **–POT** + + **AZ** + **–C** =

5. + + **S** =

6. + **–S** =

PRAYER

Dear God,
how wonderful it is to realize that
You are everywhere, all the time.
My mind cannot understand Your omnipresence,
but I thank You for being such a marvelous God.
I like the idea that You surround me and that
You love me so much You want to live within me.
Help me remember that You are always near.
Make me aware of Your Spirit helping me
when I am tempted to do wrong.
In Jesus' name, amen.

O

. . . .

GOD IS OMNISCIENT

Nothing in all creation is hidden from God's sight. Everything is uncovered and laid bare before the eyes of him to whom we must give account.

Hebrews 4:13

SMART COMPUTER

"This is strange," said Jeff. "This computer knows my name, my age, where I was born, and who my parents are. It even knows I got into a fight in second grade and failed my math test last month. Does it know everything?"

"It may seem like it," said Miss Marsh, his teacher. "Actually, when you came to kindergarten, information about you was fed into the computer. Every year teachers add more information about you. Computers are smart; they remember everything that is put into them. But I must admit, they don't know everything. Only God our heavenly Father knows everything. Only God is omniscient."

□   □   □

Understanding words

Here's another one of those "omni-" words that describes God. *Omniscient* (ahm nish' ent) means:

- all-knowing,
- having complete knowledge,
- understanding everything.

GOD KNOWS EVERYTHING

1. Fill in the missing letters to discover what the Bible says about our omniscient God.

   a. First Chronicles 28:9 says, "For the LORD searches every

   __ E __ __ __ and understands every

   M __ __ __ __ __ behind the thoughts."

   b. Job said of God, "Does he not see my ways and count my

   every __ T __ __ ?" (Job 31:4).

   c. In Psalm 33:13-14 we read, "From heaven the LORD looks down

   and sees all __ __ N __ __ __ __ ; from his dwelling

   place he watches all who live on earth."

d. Psalm 44:21 says, "Would not God have discovered it, since he knows the __ __ C __ __ __ __ of the heart?"

e. The psalmist wrote, "The LORD knows the __ __ O __ __ __ __ __ of man" (Psalm 94:11).

f. The Lord declared through His prophet, "My eyes are on all their __ __ __ S ; they are not hidden from me, nor is their __ I __ concealed from my eyes" (Jeremiah 16:17).

g. God said to His people, "But I know what is going through your __ __ N __ " (Ezekiel 11:5).

h. Daniel said to Nebuchadnezzar, "But there is a God in heaven who reveals __ __ __ __ __ __ __ __ __ " (Daniel 2:28).

2. Complete this acrostic for the word *omniscient.* Use the words you found in the Scriptures above. The letter supplied is the clue for which word fits that position in the acrostic.

```
    __ __ O __ __ __ __ __
       M __ __ __ __
    __ __ N __
       __ I __
    __ __ __ S
    __ __ __ C __ __ __ __
__ __ __ __ __ I __ __
    __ __ E __ __ __
    __ __ N __ __ __ __
       __ T __ __
```

0 123

Can you hide your feelings from God?

3. We learn from 1 Kings 8:39 that God "deal[s] with each man according to all he does, since you [God] know his

_____ (for you alone know the _____ of

_____ men)."

4. God's omniscience is clearly stated in 1 John 3:20: "For God is

greater than our _____, and he knows _____."

Can you hide yourself from God?

5. The writer of Proverbs says, "The eyes of the LORD are

_____, keeping watch on the _____ and the

_____" (Proverbs 15:3).

6. Job, the "suffering servant," wrote concerning God, "His eyes are

on the ways of men; he sees their _____ step. There is

no _____ place, no _____ shadow, where

evildoers can _____" (Job 34:21-22).

Runaways

Complete this puzzle by naming four men who tried to hide or run away from God.

1. God saw him on a ship heading for Tarshish (Jonah 1:3).

2. God saw him kill his brother (Genesis 4:9).

3. God saw him hiding in the garden (Genesis 3:8).

4. God saw him hide stolen property (Joshua 7:11,20).

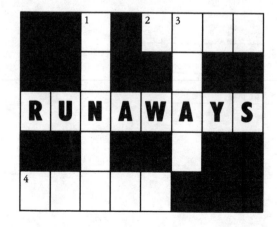

☆ APPLICATION AND PRAYER

This choral reading is taken from Psalm 139:1-12,16-18,23 in *The Living Bible*. When you read it, you'll be praising God, and you'll be reviewing God's omniscience and omnipresence.

Reader 1—solo, light or high voice
Reader 2—solo, heavy or low voice
Girls—can be one or many
Boys—can be one or many
All—everyone

All: O LORD, you have examined my heart and know everything about me.

Girls: You know when I sit or stand.

Boys: When far away you know my every thought.

Reader 1: You chart the path ahead of me, and tell me where to stop and rest.

All: Every moment, you know where I am.

Reader 2: You know what I am going to say before I even say it.

Girls: You both precede and follow me,

Boys: and place your hand of blessing on my head.

All: This is too glorious, too wonderful to believe!

Reader 1: I can *never* be lost to your Spirit!

Reader 2: I can *never* get away from my God!

Reader 1: If I go up to heaven, you are there;

Reader 2: if I go down to the place of the dead, you are there.

All: This is too glorious, too wonderful to believe!

Reader 1: If I ride the morning winds to the farthest oceans, even there your hand will guide me, your strength will support me.

Reader 2: If I try to hide in the darkness, the night becomes light around me. For even darkness cannot hide from God;

Girls: to you the night shines as bright as day.

Boys: Darkness and light are both alike to you.

All: This is too glorious, too wonderful to believe!

Reader 1: You saw me before I was born and scheduled each day of my life before I began to breathe.

Reader 2: Every day was recorded in your Book!

Girls: How precious it is, Lord, to realize that you are thinking about me constantly!

Boys: I can't even count how many times a day your thoughts turn toward me.

Girls: And when I waken in the morning, you are still thinking of me!

All: This is too glorious, too wonderful to believe!

All: Search me, O God,

Boys: and know my heart;

Girls: test my thoughts.

Boys: Point out anything you find in me that makes you sad,

Girls: and lead me along the path of everlasting life.

All: *In Jesus' name, amen.*

P

GOD IS OUR PROVIDER

But my God shall supply all your need according to his riches in glory by Christ Jesus.

Philippians 4:19, KJV

P

HOW GOD SUPPLIED NEEDS

Here are three stories involving God's miracles of provision. At the end of each story are some questions with four possible answers. Circle the letter in front of the correct answer. To be sure you chose the right answer, check it out in the Scripture passage given.

Mystery of the jugs (2 Kings 4:1-7)

"This man must be crazy," said a small boy dragging a huge clay jug down the road.

"Perhaps," said his older brother, carrying a jar on each shoulder. "But with Father dead, nothing to eat, and the landlord threatening to take our house away—I'm ready to try anything."

"It's worse than that." The small boy sniffled. "Last night when I was almost asleep, a mean man came to see Mother. He said if she doesn't pay her debts, something terrible will happen to you and me."

Mother held open the canvas door flap of their mud-brick home. The boys put the jars and jug on the dirt floor.

Looking at the crowded house, the older son said, "That's it! That's all the empty jugs and jars our neighbors could loan us."

The man of God told the widow to take her little bit of olive oil and start pouring it into the jugs.

The boys watched their mother fill every jar, jug, and cooking pot with oil. When she finished, her tiny jar had no more oil in it.

"This is a mystery," said the small boy with eyes open wide. "Where did the oil come from?"

"God supplied it," said the man of God. "Now, take the oil to the market. Sell it. And after you pay your debts, you will still have enough for everything you and your sons need."

☐   ☐   ☐

1. What would have happened to the widow's sons if she could not pay her debts?
   a. They would become slaves.
   b. They would go to prison.
   c. They would be beaten.
   d. They would die of hunger.

2. Who was this man of God who worked a miracle for this poor widow and her sons?
   d. Elijah
   e. Elisha
   f. Ezekiel
   g. Ezra

Fed by the birds (1 Kings 17:2-6)

"Now do what I tell you," God said to Elijah. "Go eastward and hide in the ravine so Queen Jezebel can't find you."

"But, Lord," said Elijah, "what will I eat?"

"Don't worry about a little thing like that," God said. "You can drink water from the brook. I will order some birds to bring you bread and meat every morning and evening until I tell you to move on."

☐   ☐   ☐

3. What was the name of the ravine where Elijah hid?
   h. Tishbe
   i. Jordan
   j. Kerith
   k. Zarephath

4. What kind of birds did God command to bring food to feed Elijah?
   h. ravens
   i. hawks
   j. eagles
   k. crows

Deadly water (2 Kings 2:18-22)

"My children are sick and dying," said a father sadly.

"My grape vines are shriveling up," a farmer said.

"It's that water from the biggest spring just outside the city. It's gone bad," said another farmer.

The city leaders discussed the serious problem. That spring was their very life. Without it . . . well, they had to do something. But what?

"Let's find Elisha. I'm sure he can help us."

Elisha threw something into the water and said, "Never again will this spring cause children to die or make your land useless. The Lord has healed these waters."

☐   ☐   ☐

5. What was the name of the city with the polluted spring?
   e. Jerusalem
   f. Samaria
   g. Bethel
   h. Jericho

6. What did Elisha throw into the polluted water?
   u. sugar
   v. salt
   w. sand
   x. spices

7. What or who made the water pure again?
   l. men
   m. Elisha
   n. magic
   o. God

On the blank spaces below, write the letters you circled for each of the above seven answers.

—— —— —— —— —— —— ——

Now unscramble them to find the Hebrew name for God.

—— —— —— —— —— —— ——

MORE OF GOD'S PROVISIONS

1. Moses wrote of God, "He defends the cause of the

   _____ and the _____, and loves the

   _____, giving him _____ and _____"
   (Deuteronomy 10:18).

2. According to Psalm 104:14, "He makes _____ grow for

   the _____, and _____ for man to

   _____—bringing forth _____ from the earth."

3. We receive comfort from the words of Isaiah 40:29: "He gives

   _____ to the _____ and increases the

   _____ of the _____."

4. Psalm 107:8-9 says, "Let them give _____ to the LORD for

   his unfailing _____ and his wonderful _____

   for men, for he satisfies the _____ and fills the

   _____ with _____ things."

☆APPLICATION

Family history is important. God told parents to pass on the story of His great deeds, so future generations would know about them.

1. Parents, tell your children about times in your early life when God supplied your needs.

2. Children, talk about some recent times when God met your needs.

3. Look back at Psalm 107:8-9. What should we do when God supplies our needs?

CHALLENGE

Let's be "word detectives." Like a detective who puts clues together to solve a mystery, you'll put letters together to form words. A person can play alone or the entire family can play together. Choose one of the attributes of God, like *provider* or *incomparable.* Each person writes this master word across the top of a sheet of paper. Divide the paper into four columns: two-letter words, three-letter words, four-letter words, five-letter words (or more).

The object of the game is to see how many words you can make by using only the letters in the master word. If two or more people are playing, you may want to set a timer for ten or fifteen minutes. When your time is up, compare your list with others in the family. Ready? For your first word, let's choose *incomparable.*

Incomparable

two-letter words	three-letter words	four-letter words	five or more

PRAYER

Dear God,
Thank You for the stories in the Bible
that tell how You provided for people
when they needed something desperately.
It makes our faith grow so we can
believe You will help us, too.
Thank You for Your promise
that You will supply all our needs
according to Your great riches and power.
[Do you have a special need now? Tell God about it.]
In Jesus' name, amen.

Q
GOD IS FOUND IN QUIETNESS

"Be still, and know that I am God."

Psalm 46:10

Q

QUIET, PLEASE!

"Be still and listen to me," said a mother to her wiggling four-year-old.

□   □   □

"No talking in the library," said the stern lady with the wire-rimmed glasses.

□   □   □

"Turn off that television. I'm talking long distance to your grandmother."

□   □   □

"Hush! Hush! Whisper who dares!
Christopher Robin is saying his prayers."

—A.A. Milne
"Vespers"

□   □   □

Evidently people need quietness in order to concentrate on listening, reading, thinking, and praying.

Understanding words

What does it mean to be still? To be quiet?

- *Still* means: without motion, little or no activity; calm, resting, not busy.
- *Quiet* means: without noise, little or no sound; peaceful, silent.

Quiet times and places

Of what do the words *quiet* and *still* make you think?

Below is a diagram of a word cluster. In the center is the word *quietness*. Spokes go from quietness to other ovals. In these ovals, print a *place* that brings quietness or stillness to you. I printed "mountains" for one. Can you think of five more?

Next, think about quiet experiences you had at these places. Write them on the spokes radiating from each of these places.

Remember how you felt? Remember what you saw?

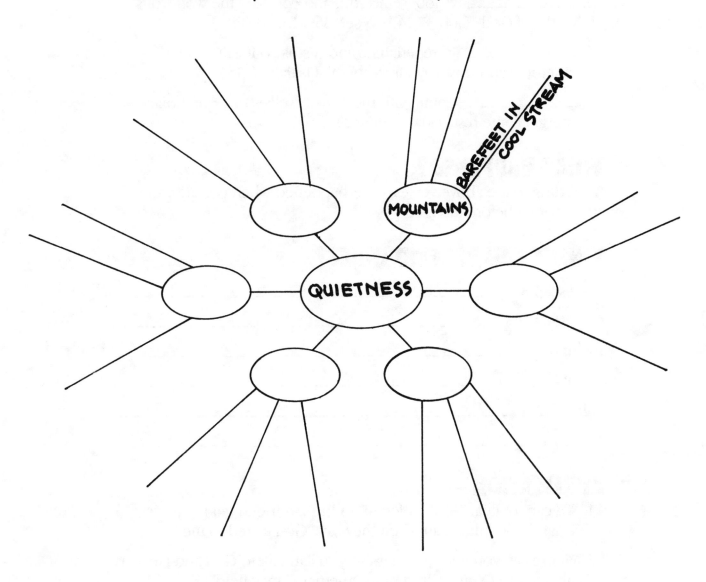

WHO SAID IT?

1. _____ "The LORD will fight for you; you need only to be still" (Exodus 14:13-14).

2. _____ "Stand still, and I will hear what the LORD will command concerning you" (Numbers 9:8, KJV).

3. _____ "But stand thou still awhile, that I may show thee the word of God" (1 Samuel 9:27, KJV).

4. _____ "O Job: stand still, and consider the wondrous works of God" (Job 37:14, KJV; see 36:1 for speaker).

5. _____ "In repentance and rest is your salvation, in quietness and trust is your strength" (Isaiah 30:15).

6. _____ "Come with me by yourselves to a quiet place and get some rest" (Mark 6:30-32).

WHAT HAPPENED?

According to the above verses, what happened when people were still or quiet before the Lord?

WHERE CAN WE FIND QUIET?

Genesis 3:8 _____

Genesis 24:63 _____

Psalm 63:6 _____

Habakkuk 2:20 _____

Luke 6:12 _____

Acts 16:13 _____

☆ APPLICATION

1. We cannot hear God's voice like a human friend talking to us. What do people mean when they say "God talked to me"?

2. Where can you find quietness so you can talk to God and He can talk to you? (Your "Cluster on Quietness" may help.)

3. Here are two ways to find quietness to worship God.
   a. Go for a walk in the park or woods. Be aware of the sights and sounds of nature. Thank God for His creation.

   b. On Sunday, sit still and listen to the organ or piano before the worship service begins. Think about God's attributes.

CHALLENGE

When life gets too busy or noisy, it's difficult to hear God's quiet voice. The world likes excitement and clashing sounds. It says, "Quietness is depressing. Who needs it!"

In this play, some famous Bible characters testify about why quietness is important to them.

Quietness on trial

Judge—in charge of the courtroom
David—king of Israel
Elijah—God's bold prophet
Jesus—the Son of God
Defender—counsel for Quietness
Prosecutor—counsel for the World
Narrator—describes characters

Scene 1—David on the stand

Narrator: As the authoritative judge pounds his gavel on his bench, everyone in the courtroom stops talking.

Judge: The court will hear case number 155 in which the World is bringing action against Quietness. The counsel for Quietness will defend the concept that "God is found in quietness." Counsel for Quietness, call your first witness to the stand.

Defender: Your Honor, I call King David to the stand.

Narrator: A dignified man in a purple robe enters the witness box. A gold crown rests on his white hair.

Defender: Are you David, the shepherd boy who became a king?

David: Yes, I am.

Defender: Do you swear to tell the truth, the whole truth, and nothing but the truth?

David: I do.

Defender: The Scriptures say you are a man after God's own heart. Does that mean you and God are on speaking terms?

David: Yes, I talk to God. And I listen, too.

Defender: How and when do you listen to God?

David: Listening to God has always been important to me. When I was a teenager, I watched my father's sheep. I was alone a lot, and it was quiet in the fields. I often sat on big rocks, played my harp, and thought about God. I wrote many poems about Him. I believe He put thoughts into my mind while I was watching the sheep.

Defender: Hmm. Putting thoughts into your mind? Can you tell about a specific time when this happened?

David: It's a shepherd's job to find grassy fields and fresh water for his sheep, to lead them safely over rugged mountain paths, and to protect them from wild animals. One day God showed me that He was like a shepherd to me. He promised to guide me and to protect me from my enemies. It was in the quietness on the mountains that God became my best friend.

Defender: Thank you. Your Honor, I have no more questions for this witness.

Judge: Does the counsel for the World wish to cross-examine?

Prosecutor: Yes, Your Honor. King David, we can see how *easy* it was for you to find God in the quietness as a lonely shepherd. But what about after you became king of Israel?

David: I needed to hear God more as a king than I did as a shepherd. I needed to know He was directing me.

Prosecutor: You were very busy ruling the country. You attended banquets and meetings, signed laws, and fought wars. With people around you continuously, when and where could you possibly find quiet time?

David: In the middle of the night. Whenever I couldn't sleep, I meditated on the Scriptures. I thought about God and praised Him. God talked to me while I lay quietly on my bed. In fact, I wrote some of my best poems during the night. Have you read my poetry collection, sir?

Prosecutor: (huffy) Of course not. I'm finished, Your Honor.

Scene 2—Elijah on the stand

Judge: Counsel for Quietness, call your next witness.

Narrator: Elijah, the bold prophet, dressed in worn leather, takes the stand. His husky voice fills the courtroom as he repeats the oath.

Defender: Are you Elijah, the man who called down fire from Heaven on top of Mount Carmel?

Elijah: I sure am. That fire burned up everything: the bull, the wood, and the water.

Defender: It's evident that God heard your prayer. What happened after that great experience?

Elijah: I was pretty depressed. Queen Jezebel was out to kill me. I was afraid. I ran to the desert, sat under a broom tree, and told God I wanted to die.

Defender: Evidently God didn't answer that prayer.

Elijah: He had other plans. After I rested, God sent me bread and water. Then I hiked for forty days and nights. At Mount Horeb, I went into a cave and spent the night.

Defender: That sounds like a quiet place. Did God talk to you in the cave?

Elijah: God asked me what I was doing there. I told Him I was His only prophet left and I was hiding because the queen planned to kill me.

Defender: What did God say to that?

Elijah: He told me to stand on the mountain and wait for Him.

Defender: The Scriptures say that a great and powerful wind tore the mountains apart and shattered the rocks.

Elijah: I stood trembling in the mouth of the cave. I watched and waited, but God was not in the wind.

Defender: After the wind, there was an earthquake.

Elijah: I shook as the rocks tumbled down the mountainside, but God was not in the earthquake.

Defender: After the earthquake, there was a fire.

Elijah: Those flames were hot. They burned all the trees in front of the cave, but God was not in the fire.

Defender: What came after the fire?

Elijah: I heard a whisper. This was more terrifying than the wind or earthquake or fire. I pulled my cloak over my face and came out of the cave.

Defender: And did God speak to you then?

Elijah: In a kind voice, God told me I wasn't His only prophet left. There were still seven thousand others who were faithful to Him. Then He gave me my next assignment.

Defender: I have no further questions, Your Honor.

Judge: Does the counsel for the World wish to cross-examine?

Prosecutor: Yes, Your Honor. Mr. Elijah, people call you the great champion of God. But from what I hear, you're just a noisy preacher.

Elijah: Strange as it may seem, I like quietness. I always heard God speaking to me when I was alone and quiet.

Prosecutor: You told about one time, but once isn't much proof.

Elijah: On another occasion, I was hiding in a ravine during the three-year drought. I heard God speaking to me then.

Prosecutor: What did God say?

Elijah: He told me to go to Zarephath and stay with a widow and her son until the famine was over.

Prosecutor: Why was quietness necessary for that?

Elijah: God always gave me my marching orders. I might not have heard Him in a noisy place.

Prosecutor: Do you expect people to believe that a bellowing prophet like you hears God in quietness?

Elijah: It doesn't matter what others believe. I know where I hear God. I think I'll leave this noisy courtroom. I sure can't hear God here.

Prosecutor: No further questions.

Scene 3—Jesus on the stand

Narrator: The last witness is a man with a kind face and a warm smile. As He lifts His hand to take the oath, the jury sees a round scar in His palm.

Defender: Are You Jesus Christ, the Son of the living God?

Jesus: Yes, I am.

Defender: You led a very busy life on earth. Tell the jury how You managed to find a quiet time or place so God could speak to You.

Jesus: My days lasted from daybreak to dark. I was busy preaching, teaching, and working miracles. But I still found time to get alone and talk with My Father. I often went into the hills early in the morning while birds were still singing.

Defender: But You're the Son of God. Why would You seek a quiet place to talk to *Your* Father?

Jesus: I love people, but I love My Father more. Sometimes I went to the mountains and stayed all night so I could be alone with God. I needed direction and encouragment. I needed to hear Him say, "I love You, My Son. You are pleasing Me."

Defender: I have no further questions, Your Honor.

Judge: Does the counsel for the World wish to cross-examine?

Prosecutor: Yes, Your Honor. (turning angrily to Jesus) Are You saying that God can only talk to people when they are quiet? Like in the desert or mountains, or early in the morning, or in the middle of the night? I thought Your God was all-powerful. I thought He could do anything.

Jesus: God is found in quietness because that's when it's easiest for people to listen. God can speak anytime. He can speak in the thunder or the fire, in a noisy stadium or on a city street. But His voice is usually crowded out and man cannot hear Him.

Prosecutor: Is that so important?

Jesus: It was to Me. People must be still to hear God speaking, to receive His directions for their daily lives, and to hear His words of love and encouragement.

Prosecutor: (disgustedly) I have no further questions.

Judge: All witnesses have testified. The jury is dismissed. Please return when you have reached a verdict.

□   □   □

Discussion

Your family is the jury.
   1. Discuss the witnesses.
      a. How would you describe their characters?

      b. What type of reputation do they have?

   2. Discuss the testimonies of the three witnesses.
      a. Why were their stories believable?

      b. In what ways were they convincing?

   3. What is your verdict? Is God found in quietness?

Message from Jesus

In the spaces following each definition, write the correct word. Transfer only the numbered letters to their matching squares in the puzzle below. If you fill each square correctly, you can read a message from Jesus about how to find quiet time with God.

1. Sixty minutes
$\overline{\quad}\ \overline{\quad}\ \overline{\quad}\ \overline{\quad}$
2 13 7 22

2. Having little money
$\overline{\quad}\ \overline{\quad}\ \overline{\quad}\ \overline{\quad}$
41 46 6 9

3. Our planet
$\overline{\quad}\ \overline{\quad}\ \overline{\quad}\ \overline{\quad}\ \overline{\quad}$
- 52 56 16 32

4. Opposite of lost
$\overline{\quad}\ \overline{\quad}\ \overline{\quad}\ \overline{\quad}\ \overline{\quad}$
51 23 20 4 -

5. Poem or verse
$\overline{\quad}\ \overline{\quad}\ \overline{\quad}\ \overline{\quad}\ \overline{\quad}\ \overline{\quad}$
8 48 3 31 50 5

6. The day before today
$\overline{\quad}\ \overline{\quad}\ \overline{\quad}\ \overline{\quad}\ \overline{\quad}\ \overline{\quad}\ \overline{\quad}\ \overline{\quad}\ \overline{\quad}$
47 33 - 53 55 21 34 10 44

7. Kind and compassionate
$\overline{\quad}\ \overline{\quad}\ \overline{\quad}\ \overline{\quad}\ \overline{\quad}\ \overline{\quad}\ \overline{\quad}\ \overline{\quad}$
12 37 43 26 14 19 49 29

8. Jesus rode this animal
$\overline{\quad}\ \overline{\quad}\ \overline{\quad}\ \overline{\quad}\ \overline{\quad}\ \overline{\quad}$
40 28 39 - 30 11

9. A grown-up girl
$\overline{\quad}\ \overline{\quad}\ \overline{\quad}\ \overline{\quad}\ \overline{\quad}$
1 36 25 38 15

10. The part of a plant that grows downward
$\overline{\quad}\ \overline{\quad}\ \overline{\quad}\ \overline{\quad}$
42 35 17 45

11. Belonging to God; sacred
$\overline{\quad}\ \overline{\quad}\ \overline{\quad}\ \overline{\quad}$
54 24 27 18

1	2	3	4		5	6	7		8	9	10	11	
12	13		14	15	16	17		18	19	20	21		22	23	24	25
			26	27	28	29	30		31	32	33		34	35	36	37
				38	39	40		41	42	43	44	
			45	46		47	48	49	50		51	52	53	54	55	56

Matthew 6:6

PRAYER

Write your own prayer, praising God for the way He talked to David, Elijah, and Jesus. Thank Him for times when He talks to you. Ask Him to help you find more quiet times so you can hear His voice and learn to know Him better.

R

GOD IS OUR REFUGE

God is our refuge and strength, an
ever-present help in trouble.

Psalm 46:1

A REFUGE FOR ANIMALS

Teddie loved the outdoors and he loved books. He spent a lot of time studying birds and plants and animals. His mother complained when she found dead birds and mice in his dresser drawers.

He never lost his love for nature even after he became President of the United States.

One day Teddie heard that the brown pelicans were disappearing from their nesting land, and he became concerned. In 1903, he declared that Pelican Island, off the east coast of Florida, would be protected by the United States government. Now the pelicans could be born and live in safety. He called it a wildlife refuge.

This was the beginning of the National Wildlife Refuge System. Today the United States government has set aside 410 refuges covering about 89 million acres of land. There birds, fish, and animals can live safely in their natural habitats. There they are protected from people who might carelessly hurt or destroy them.

Can you name this president? The answer is printed upside down on the bottom of this page.

A REFUGE FOR PEOPLE

Old Testament writers often compared God to familiar things, so people could understand who God is and what God does for them. Many Scriptures describe God as a *refuge* (a shelter or protection from danger or trouble).

Here are eight objects that each picture God as a different kind of refuge. Write the matching Scripture under each object.

Deuteronomy 33:27   Psalm 91:4   Isaiah 25:4
Psalm 9:9   Psalm 119:114   Jeremiah 16:19
Psalm 71:3   Proverbs 18:10

(Answer: *Theodore Roosevelt* was the twenty-sixth president, from 1901-1909.)

146 R

1._____ 2._____

3._____ 4._____

5._____ 6._____

7._____ 8._____

R¹⁴⁷

☆ APPLICATION

1. When and where have you found a refuge from a storm? From the sun? From danger?

2. Read Psalm 91:1-2.

   a. How can you "dwell in the shelter of the Most High"?

   b. What else should you do in times of trouble?

   c. What promise is given if you do those two things?

CHALLENGE

1. Color-code these Scriptures:
   * 2 Samuel 22:2-3
   * Psalm 57:1
   * Psalm 62:6-8
   * Psalm 94:22

2. Choose one of the above verses to memorize.

A message in Morse code

In 1840, Samuel Morse designed a code using dots, dashes, and spaces to send messages by telegraph within the United States and Canada.

Later the international Morse code was developed and used between countries. It is still used today on shortwave radio. The code S O S . . . _ _ _ . . . is used when people need help.

A . _	N _ .	1 . _ _ _ _	period . _ . _ . _
B _ . . .	O _ _ _	2 . . _ _ _	comma _ _ . . _ _
C _ . _ .	P . _ _ .	3 . . . _ _	colon _ _ _ . . .
D _ . .	Q _ _ . _	4 . . . . _	semicolon _ . _ . _ .
E .	R . _ .	5	quotation mark . _ . . _ .
F . . _ .	S . . .	6 _	question mark . . _ _ . .
G _ _ .	T _	7 _ _ . . .	start _ . _
H	U . . _	8 _ _ _ . .	wait . _ . . .
I . .	V . . . _	9 _ _ _ _ .	end of message . _ . _ .
J . _ _ _	W . _ _	0 _ _ _ _ _	
K _ . _	X _ . . _		
L . _ . .	Y _ . _ _		
M _ _	Z _ _ . .		

Use the international Morse code to decipher the following message. It will be a comfort to you when you need shelter or protection. When you see a double line, use punctuation or a command.

— · —   — — ·   — — —   — · ·

· ·   · · ·   — —   — · — —

· — ·   ·   · · — ·   —

· · —   — — ·   ·   · — · — ·

—   · · · ·   · ·   · · ·   · ·

— · —   — ·   — — —   · — —   · — · — ·   · — · · ·

· · · ·   ·

· — —   · ·   · — · ·   · — · ·

— · · ·   ·

· — —   · ·   —   · · · ·

— —   ·   — — · — —

· — —   · · · ·   ·   · — ·

·   · · · —   ·   · — ·

· ·   — — ·   — — —   · — · — ·   · — · — ·

PRAYER

Dear heavenly Father,
I love nature and everything You created.
Thank You for people who have planned for and
take care of refuges for birds and animals and trees.
And, Lord, I'm glad to know that You are my refuge.
Thank You for Your promise
to be my shelter and protection from trouble.
Help me to trust in You.
You are a great and good God.
Thank You for helping me learn more about You.
In Jesus' name, amen.

S

· · · · · · · · · · · · · ·

GOD IS
SOVEREIGN

And we know that in all things God
works for the good of those who
love him.

Romans 8:28

SUNSHINE AFTER THE STORM

Jessica pressed the pink salmon egg on the fishhook. "I bet I catch a trout before you do, Dad."

"You're willing to bet with an experienced fisherman?" her father laughed as he cast his line into the mountain stream.

The sky was blue and cloudless. For the first time in ages, Jessica had her dad all to herself.

They hiked the stream, fishing as they went. At noon they ate lunch in an aspen grove. Dad told jokes; Jessica laughed.

While they ate, the wind blew in some dark clouds.

"It looks like there's a storm coming," said Dad. "Maybe we should. . . ."

"Who's afraid of a little shower? Come on." She pulled on his arm. "Let's each catch one more trout."

But it was more than an afternoon shower. Lightning flashed, thunder rumbled, and giant drops of rain poured down like Niagara Falls.

Jessica shook her fist at the storm. Her day was ruined.

In a nearby cave, wet and shivering, she huddled next to her dad. She felt his strong arm pull her close.

"Since we can't fish, can we talk?" she asked timidly.

"You mean tell jokes?"

"No, I mean serious stuff."

"About what?"

"You and me, my feelings."

Dad spread his poncho on the ground and they sat down. Jessica told how her brother, Jeff, got to go everywhere with Dad, how she felt left out, and how unfair she was always treated. Even today the storm proved that.

Then Dad told Jessica that he thought she didn't want to be with him, that she only cared about her friends.

While the clouds poured out their rain, father and daughter poured out their hearts.

When the sun appeared, Jessica stood up. "I was mad because I thought the storm had ruined my day, but it didn't. It turned out great."

□   □   □

Like a director working backstage, God is working behind the scenes in our lives. He is in charge. He can turn bad into good; storms into sunshine. God can work all things out for our good and His glory because He is *sovereign* (sahv' wren).

Can you find a small word in *sovereign* that means to rule or be in control?

God has supreme authority over everything and everybody. Revelation 3:7 says, "What he _____ no one can _____, and what he _____ no one can _____."

GOD IS IN COMPLETE CONTROL

1. Search the following Scriptures and write down what God has control over.

   Daniel 2:21

   a. _____

   b. _____

   Daniel 4:35

   a. _____

   b. _____

   Acts 17:26

   a. _____

   b. _____

When God created people, He gave them the freedom to make their own choices. But, like a farmer who puts a gate in his pasture fence so he can get in, God left an opening into our lives so He could reach through and work out His plan.

God intervenes for a purpose.
God can intervene—*come between you and your problems*—to turn things around for your good. The following Scriptures are evidence of this.

2. According to Genesis 50:20, Joseph said to his brothers, "You intended to _____ me, but God intended it for _____ to _____ what is now being _____, the saving of many lives."

3. We read the prophet's message from God in Isaiah 48:17: "I am the LORD your God, who _____ you what is _____ for you, who _____ you in the _____ you _____ go."

4. And again in Isaiah 50:9, God's control is made clear: "It is the Sovereign LORD who _____ me."

God interferes in the plans of enemies.

Like a lineman in football who runs interference *to block and protect* the player with the ball, so God blocks and protects those who love Him, from the attack of the enemy.

5. Read the Scriptures below and write in the appropriate spaces who God protected and who the enemy was.

	GOD PROTECTED	from	THE ENEMY
1 Samuel 23:14-15			
Job 1:9-12			
John 7:28-30			

CHALLENGE

In 605 BC, the Jews were taken to Babylon as prisoners of war. Seventy years later, God sent them back to Jerusalem to rebuild the Temple, the city, and the walls.

But seventy years is a long time. Many Jews decided to stay in Persia where they were born. This was true of Mordecai and his young cousin Esther. This play will show how God intervened and carried out His plan for His people.

An orphan in royal robes
The book of Esther

Esther—a Jewish orphan who became a Persian queen
Mordecai—Esther's foster father and a royal official
Xerxes—the king of Persia (pronounced Zurk' seez)
Haman—the prime minister who hated the Jews
Hathach—Esther's adviser
Maiden—Esther's maidservant
Zeresh—wife of Haman
Narrator—storyteller

Scene 1—Home of Mordecai

Esther: At the market today, I heard women whispering about Queen Vashti. They said the king asked her to his banquet, but she refused. Now the king is angry. Is that true?

Mordecai: Yes, and Vashti is no longer the queen.

Esther: Who will be the new queen?

Mordecai: From all over the Persian empire, the most beautiful young women are to be brought to the palace here in Susa so the king can choose the one he likes best.

Esther: That will be a difficult decision.

Mordecai: You've grown up to be a charming, lovely lady, Esther. You are just as beautiful on the inside as you are on the outside. I'm sure you would please the king.

Esther: (gasping) Me?

Mordecai: I'm going to take you to the harem where all the women of the king's household live. I'll introduce you to Hegai. He's in charge.

Esther: Does he know we're cousins? Does he know you've been a father to me since my parents died?

Mordecai: No. And you mustn't tell anyone we're related or that we're Jews. I have a good job. I might lose it if this were known.

Esther: I'll keep our secret, Mordecai. But I'm frightened. I don't know anything about royalty—except what you've told me because of your job at the palace.

Mordecai: Don't worry. All of the contestants will be trained in royal etiquette before they are sent to the king.

Narrator: Hegai welcomed Esther, along with hundreds of women from all over the Persian empire.

Hegai liked Esther immediately. She was trim and shapely. Her dark eyes sparkled; her long black hair glistened. She was kind and friendly to everyone. Hegai assigned her the best rooms in the harem and gave her seven maids to serve her.

For a year the young women received daily beauty treatments, ate special foods, and learned how to walk and talk and act like a queen. When twelve months passed, each young woman spent time with King Xerxes. He liked Esther the best and chose her to be his queen.

S155

Scene 2—Queen Esther's palace

Narrator: For four years Esther kept her secret. Then one day she received bad news from Mordecai.

Hathach: (bowing) Yes, Queen Esther. What can I do for you?

Esther: The king's life is in danger. Mordecai overheard two of the palace guards planning to kill the king. You must warn the king. Tell him Mordecai uncovered the plan.

Narrator: The king investigated and found it was true. The two men were hanged. The royal secretary wrote down all the details in the history scrolls.

Life in Susa was peaceful, until one day the king appointed a man named Haman to be his prime minister.

Scene 3—Home of Haman

Haman: Tonight, my dear wife, I am both glad and mad.

Zeresh: Tell me the good news first.

Haman: Because I'm so clever, I've been promoted. You're looking at the most powerful man in the empire, next to the king himself.

Zeresh: (pleased) That makes me a very important wife. With such good news, how could you be mad?

Haman: The king commanded all the royal officials to honor me. Those at the gate kneel in the dust when I pass in and out, but there is one who will not bow to me.

Zeresh: Who is this man who shows no respect?

Haman: It's Mordecai. I've heard he's a Jew.

Zeresh: And you know that Jews bow only to their God. What will you do?

Haman: (shouting) I've got to get rid of him. In fact, I'll think of a reason to have all the Jews killed.

Narrator: That night Haman lay awake, thinking of ways he could carry out his evil plan.

Scene 4—King's throne room, next morning

Haman: O king, I've discovered a problem in your kingdom.

Xerxes: Tell me about it.

Haman: There are certain people scattered throughout your countries who follow their own customs and obey their own laws instead of your laws. This is not good for your kingdom.

Xerxes: You're right. What shall we do?

Haman: We could destroy these troublemakers. I'll offer twenty million dollars to the soldiers who do it.

Xerxes: I don't need your money, but you can write a new law. Stamp it with my signet ring to show I approve it. When will this happen?

Haman: We'll cast the pur, and let the gods select the date.

Narrator: The pur (like dice) were thrown and fell on the month of Adar. Haman had twelve months to make his plans. Copies of the law were sent throughout the Persian empire, which included Jerusalem. All the Jews would be destroyed. God's people would be annihilated from the earth.

Scene 5—Queen Esther's palace

Esther: (pacing back and forth) Where is Mordecai? I haven't seen him in the courtyard for several days.

Maiden: He can't come into the palace grounds, because he's wearing that scratchy sackcloth around his hips. His head and chest are covered with ashes. He's weeping and walking back and forth outside the gate. In fact, all the Jews in Susa are just as sad and gloomy as he is.

Esther: Why? What can this mean?

Maiden: Hathach is talking to Mordecai. He'll be back soon.

Narrator: When Hathach returned, he told Esther the whole story, and that all Jews were going to be killed.

Hathach: Mordecai said you must go to the king and beg for mercy. You must plead with him to save your people.

Esther: If I go to the king without being invited, I shall be put to death.

Hathach: There's one exception to the law. If the king holds out his gold scepter to you, your life will be spared.

Esther: But I haven't seen the king for thirty days. He may be unhappy with me. I could die for this. Does Mordecai know that?

Hathach: He knows. He said to tell you, "Do you think you will escape just because you live in the king's palace?" He said to think about this: "Perhaps you have become the queen of Persia for this very reason."

Esther: Give Mordecai this message: "Tell all the Jews in Susa to fast for me. After I and my maidens fast for three days, I'll go to the king, even though it is against the law. And if I perish, I perish."

Scene 6—King's throne room

Narrator: On the third day, dressed in her royal robes, Esther went to the king. When he saw her standing in the court, he was surprised and very pleased. He held out his gold scepter.

Xerxes: What do you want, Esther? It must be important. Whatever it is, I'll give it to you—even if it's half my kingdom.

Esther: Your Majesty, I have planned a wonderful banquet. I would like for you to come and bring Haman with you.

Narrator: At the banquet, Esther made a second request. She invited the king and Haman to another feast the next night. They both promised to be there. After the banquet, Haman hurried home to tell his wife the news.

Scene 7—Home of Haman

Haman: Tonight I was the only person invited to dine with the king and queen. And that's not all. She invited me again tomorrow night.

Zeresh: But my intuition tells me that something is wrong.

Haman: It's that Jew. Whenever I see Mordecai sitting at the king's gate, I boil inside.

Zeresh: Have a gallows built, seventy-five feet high. Ask the king to hang Mordecai on it.

Narrator: Haman liked the idea and ordered men to build the gallows in his own front yard.

Meanwhile, the king couldn't sleep, so he ordered his secretary to bring the scrolls of the historical records and read to him. The secretary read the story of how Mordecai warned the king about the plot to kill him. When the king discovered that Mordecai had never been rewarded, he made plans to honor him the next day.

Scene 8—Queen's banquet hall

Narrator: While the king and Haman were feasting with Queen Esther at the second banquet, the king asked for her request.

Esther: If I please you, and if you really love me, your Majesty, please save my life and the lives of my people.

Xerxes: What do you mean?

Esther: I and all my people are going to be killed.

Xerxes: My queen? Where is the man who plans such a horrible thing?

Esther: He sits at my table tonight. This evil man is Haman.

Narrator: Full of rage, the king ordered Haman to be hanged on the gallows prepared for Mordecai.

Scene 9—King's throne room

Narrator: A few days later, Mordecai went with Esther to see the king. Again she pleaded for her people.

Xerxes: The law I have written cannot be changed, but I can write another law. I'll give all Jews the right to protect themselves. Without fear of punishment, they may kill anyone who tries to kill them.

Narrator: Because Haman had trusted in the dice, the Jews had twelve months to prepare for the attack. They were so well prepared that no one would fight against them. Through Esther, God saved the entire Jewish nation.

□　　□　　□

Discussion

Proverbs 21:1 says, "The king's heart is in the hand of the LORD; he directs it like a watercourse wherever he pleases."

1. How did God intervene, directing the king's heart and mind?

2. How did He interfere in enemy plans?

3. How did He direct Esther?

☆APPLICATION

1. When have you been aware of God's working behind the scenes or intervening in your life? Perhaps during an accident, an illness, a problem, a relationship, or routine chores?

2. Watch for God's work in your everyday life. The more thoughtfully you watch, the more you will see. And the more you see, the more you will love our Sovereign God.

PRAYER

Sovereign God,
You are in charge of everything, including me.
I'm glad to know You have a plan for my life,
and that You love me so much You work out all my problems—
even tiny ones—for my own good.
Thanks for working in my life, even when I don't know it.
Help me to watch carefully and thoughtfully
so I can become more aware of how You work in my life.
In Jesus' name, amen.

T

GOD IS TRUE

"He who sent me is true. You do
not know him, but I know him
because I am from him and he sent
me."

John 7:28-29

WHAT DOES TRUE MEAN?

"Who can give me a definition for true?" asked the teacher.

"Not false," said Alan. "Like in a true/false test."

"That's true." The teacher smiled. "True means correct or accurate. That's one definition. True also means faithful."

"Faithful?" Alan looked puzzled. "Like what?"

"Has anyone been to Yellowstone National Park in Wyoming?"

"I have," said Tami. "When I was small, my family went on a camping trip. I saw that famous fountain that spits hot water high into the air, but I forgot what it's called."

"That geyser is called Old Faithful," said the teacher.

"How did it get that name?" asked Alan.

"Every sixty-five minutes, the geyser erupts. For about four minutes it shoots water and steam, sometimes over one-hundred feet high. People have been recording these eruptions for over eighty years. In all that time, Old Faithful has not missed one eruption."

"So?" Alan shrugged his shoulders. "Is that different from other geysers?"

"Most geysers are not dependable. No one really knows when they'll go off again. It might be hours, days, or even months."

"I got it," said Alan. "True means faithful. And faithful means you can count on it. Like the sun coming up every morning and going down every night."

The teacher nodded. "Now we know two examples of faithfulness."

□   □   □

That's what Jesus meant when He said, "God is true." You can count on God. He is faithful. He is worthy to be trusted.

God is faithful.

1. David wrote in Psalm 36:5, "Your love, O LORD, reaches to the

   heavens, your _____ to the _____."

2. Psalm 146:6 gives praise to the Lord, to "the _____ of heaven and earth, the sea, and everything in them—the

   _____, who remains faithful _____."

Comparing God's faithfulness

Read Hosea 6:3-4.

3. To what three things in nature is God compared?

a. _____

b. _____

c. _____

4. What two things are people compared to?

a. _____

b. _____

Synonyms for faithfulness

5. Match the Scripture with the correct speaker and synonym (or phrase) meaning true and faithful.

	WHO SAID IT?	SYNONYMS FOR FAITHFUL
Deuteronomy 7:9	Levites	Not one word has failed
Joshua 21:45	Paul	Every promise was fulfilled
2 Samuel 7:28	Moses	He will do it
1 Kings 8:56	Jesus	Keeps His covenant of love
Nehemiah 9:8	Joshua	Kept Your promise
John 8:26	Solomon	Trustworthy
1 Thessalonians 5:24	David	Reliable

CHALLENGE

Someone may say, "I know God was faithful to the Hebrews, but what does His faithfulness mean to me? Will His promises still come true today?" Here's a play within a story that answers those questions.

Drugs and dreams and promises

Walking home from school one afternoon, Alan picked up a handful of stones. He pitched them at a stop sign.

Clang! Clang! Clang!

"What's that all about?" asked Tami. "You got a problem?"

"Yeh, a big one. What would you do if the gang tried to get you to do drugs?" Alan asked.

"I'd just say no!"

"It's not that easy. They keep bugging me all the time. I don't want to, but I'm afraid one of these days I'll do it."

"I'd pray real hard and quote that verse I memorized about how God promised to help me when I'm tempted to do wrong."

"Do you really believe that stuff about God being true and faithful?"

"I'd sure give it a try. If God kept His promises to Moses and Joshua and David, I bet He'd keep His promise to us, too." Tami turned toward her house. "See you tomorrow."

That night, Alan was still thinking about the gang when he brushed his teeth. *Promises! That was thousands of years ago. Besides, Joshua and David didn't have guys pestering them to do drugs.*

Alan tossed and turned all night, dreaming wild dreams. In his dreams he faced the same problem he had in real life—the gang and drugs.

In one dream Alan was sitting in an auditorium waiting for a play to begin. When the curtains opened, Alan recognized the boy in the center of the stage. It was him.

□   □   □

Alan—a sixth grader
David—king of Israel
Joshua—Old Testament general
Narrator—the storyteller

Narrator: Once upon a time, a kid named Alan was walking down a dark alley when he came face to face with three guys from the Pill Gang. In each hand they carried red and blue pills as big as golf balls. Alan tried to run, but two guys grabbed him, and the third one started shoving a pill down his throat.

Alan: (shouting) No! No! I don't wanna do drugs.

Narrator: Suddenly, the guys dropped him. Staring at something behind Alan, they slowly backed out of the alley. When Alan turned, he saw two men with drawn swords flashing in the moonlight. The men were soldiers wearing ancient armor. They looked like warriors from . . . *Bible times.*

Alan: (big sigh) I don't know who you are, but you showed up just in time.

Narrator: The two soldiers pulled Alan to his feet. The handsome one spoke first.

David: I'm King David.

Joshua: And I'm General Joshua. We'd better walk you home.

Narrator: Alan had heard about these famous warriors. He felt safe walking between them.

Alan: I've been wanting to ask you guys some questions. Would this be a good time?

Joshua: No time like the present.

Alan: I'm having some trouble believing all that business about the faithfulness of God. Did God really keep all those promises He made to you guys?

David: General, you go first. You lived long before I did.

Joshua: Well, Alan, before I answer your question, let me tell you about a few experiences I had. After Moses died, God put me in charge of the Hebrew people. It was my job to take them safely into the Promised Land, but first we had to fight the Canaanites.

Alan: Were you scared?

Joshua: About as scared as you are of the gang and their drugs. I didn't have much of an organized army. Remember, we'd been wandering around in the wilderness for forty years. God knew I was scared, so He gave me a promise. I memorized it so I could remind myself, and God, about it when I needed help.

Alan: What was it? The promise, I mean.

Narrator: Joshua stroked his long white beard.

Joshua: Let's see if I can remember. It went something like this: No one will be able to stand up against you all the days of your life. I'll help you just like I did Moses. I'll never leave you or forsake you. Don't be terrified. Don't be discouraged, because I—the Lord your God—will be with you wherever you go. [See Joshua 1:5,9.]

Alan: Did the promise work? I mean, did God really go with you?

Joshua: Every time. Once God hurled hailstones down from the sky. That hail killed more Amorites than all my men with their swords. God fought for me just like He promised. Another time my small army was way outnumbered. Can you believe this? We won even when the count was a thousand enemies to one of us.

Alan: Sounds like some of the television shows I've seen.

Joshua: God worked all kinds of miracles for us. I'll never forget how those walls around Jericho toppled over. God gave me the plan, and He promised we'd capture the city.

Alan: Really?

Joshua: Yes. My army and all the men, women, and children marched around the city once a day for six days. We followed seven priests blowing seven trumpets made of ram's horns. Behind them came the Ark of the Covenant.

Alan: The Canaanites must have thought you were crazy.

Joshua: Perhaps. But we didn't care. We knew God would keep His promise. On the seventh day, we marched around seven times. When I gave the signal, the trumpets blasted the air and all the people shouted.

Alan: What happened next?

Joshua: The rock walls collapsed. They toppled over like a tower of children's blocks. The soldiers climbed over the rocks and charged into the city. We took the city just like God said we would.

Alan: It's hard to believe that story.

Joshua: Not for me. I was there, and I can testify that every promise God ever made came true. Not a single one failed.

Alan: What about you, King David?

David: For forty years I was king of Israel. I guess I'm known as the warrior king. I led my armies into many battles. And I must tell you, God *is* trustworthy. He made lots of promises to me and every one came true.

Alan: What was the best promise?

David: The best one? Hmm.

Narrator: Now it was David's time to think. He took off his crown and scratched his head.

David: Well, the Lord gave me victory everywhere I went. But two very special promises He made to me were that my son would become king and that my throne would last forever.

Alan: Was that Solomon?

David: Right! My son Solomon was king, and he built God the most beautiful temple in all the world.

Alan: What about the promise that your throne would last forever? You died and Solomon died. So, how could that ever come true?

David: The greatest promise did come true and is still true to this day.

Alan: I don't understand. Someone in your family is still a king?

David: That's true. If you read chapter one of Matthew, you'll find the genealogy of Jesus.

Alan: You mean Jesus' family tree?

David: Right! Jesus was born into the family of Joseph and Mary. If you trace Joseph's relatives back, you'll find he actually came from the family of Solomon and David—that's me. I'm about the twenty-seventh great-grandfather of Joseph.

Alan: I didn't know that. Did you . . . ?

David: Let me finish. While Jesus was on earth, He was the King of the Jews. But there's more. Someday He's coming back to earth to set up His Kingdom. And that Kingdom will last forever and ever.

Alan: Wow! What a promise.

Joshua: King David, I hate to interrupt you, but we've got to be going.

David: Goodbye, Alan.

Alan: Bye. Thanks for your help.

Joshua: I hope you find a promise you can count on.

Alan: I think I already have.

☐   ☐   ☐

Alan opened his eyes. The moon was shining on his face. He smiled as he thought about his dream. *Yep! I have a promise, the one I memorized last week: "But the Lord is faithful, and he will strengthen and protect you from the evil one"* (2 Thessalonians 3:3). Alan rolled over, punched his pillow, and fell asleep again.

☐   ☐   ☐

Discussion

1. Dreams are fun to talk about. Have you ever dreamed about your problems like Alan did? Tell your family about one dream.

2. What did God promise Joshua? (See Joshua 23:14.)

3. Talk about three times that God kept His promise to Joshua.

4. What was David's greatest promise? Can you explain how it comes true?

☆APPLICATION

1. Recall and discuss times when God's promises were true for your family.

2. Here are two promises you can memorize: 1 Corinthians 10:13 and 2 Thessalonians 3:3. When God fulfills these promises, take note of it and don't forget to praise Him!

3. One way to help you stay out of trouble is to make right choices regarding the friends you are with, the things you do, and the places you go.

A maze of choices

Life can often seem to be a maze. Making the right choices in life will help keep you out of trouble. Below is a "maze of choices." Start in the center, and see if you can find the path to the rainbow. If you end up facing a "temptation," go back to the center and start over.

PRAYER

Write a prayer, telling God how wonderful He is. Thank Him for promises that have come true in your life. Thank Him for promises He is giving you for the future. Ask Him for inner strength so you can make right choices. Ask Him to make you aware of His presence, His faithfulness, and His promises.

U
· · · · · · · · · · · · ·
GOD IS
UNCHANGEABLE

"I the LORD do not change."

Malachi 3:6

U

An old proverb says, "There is only one thing you can count on in this life, and that is change."

Let's talk about things that change.

Things that change form

Draw a line *from* each item in the center of the circle *to* the item on the outer edge of the circle that shows what new form each thing changes into.

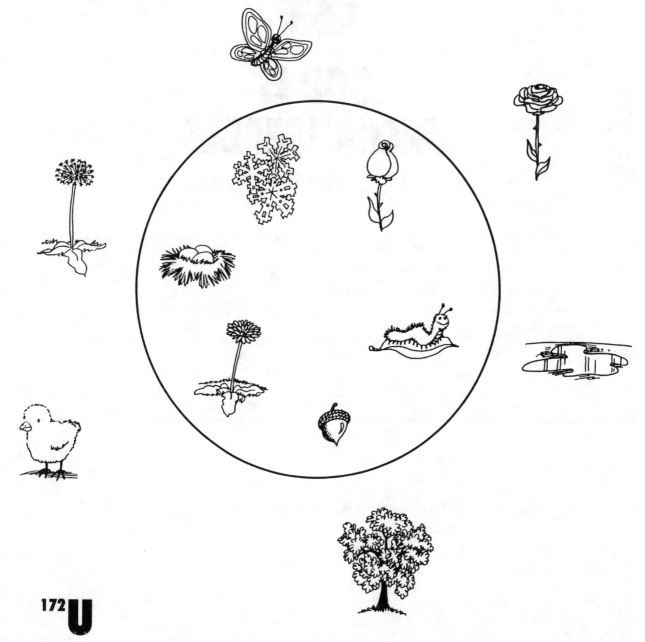

THINGS THAT CHANGE SHAPE OR SIZE

Can you solve these riddles?

1. A white or gray mass of raindrops floating above the earth.

   _____

2. A mountain puffing smoke and fire, and spitting up melted rock.

   _____

3. A mound of loose sand heaped up by the wind. _____

4. A land covered with trees destroyed by fire. _____

5. Water flowing to the sea flooded by melting snows.

   _____

6. A calf becomes a _____ and a fawn becomes a

   _____. These are _____.

7. A boy becomes a _____ and a girl becomes a

   _____. These are _____.

A riddle game

Can you make up riddles *about change* to ask family members? Try these subjects:

1. Things that wear out.

2. Things that change temperature.

3. Things that change in appearance (size, shape, color).

4. Things that die.

5. Things that can't be touched (habits, moods).

It appears that changes happen every day to every one. But, wait a minute, there is One who *never* changes!

GOD DOES NOT CHANGE

1. Two Scriptures contrast God with something that changes. Read them and find out what God is *not* like.

   James 1:17 _____

   1 Samuel 15:29 _____

Pictures of change

Our 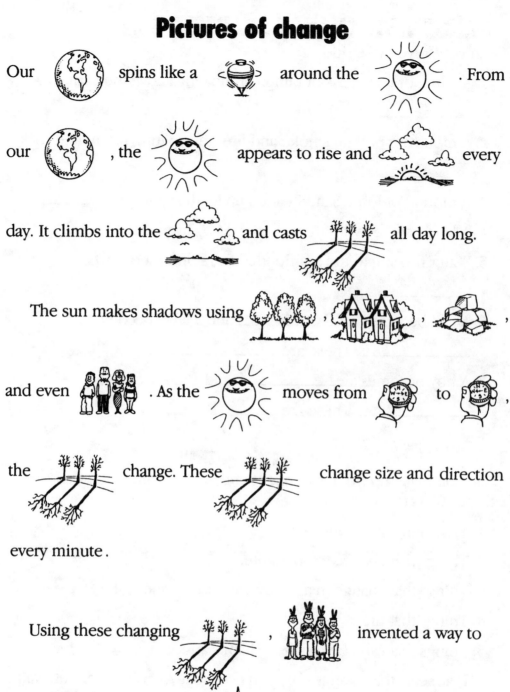 spins like a around the . From our , the appears to rise and every day. It climbs into the and casts all day long.

The sun makes shadows using , , , and even . As the moves from to , the change. These change size and direction every minute.

Using these changing 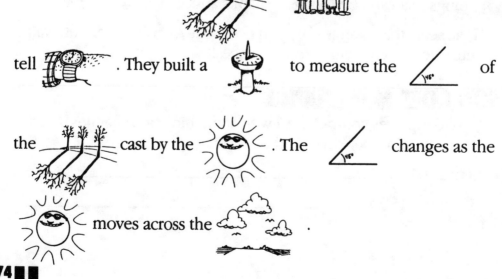 , invented a way to tell . They built a to measure the of the cast by the . The changes as the moves across the .

Shadows change, but God is not like shifting

Man changes, but God is not like inconsistent

God's plans do not change.

2. Psalm 33:11 says, "But the _____ of the LORD stand

_____ forever, the _____ of his

_____ through all _____."

God's words do not change.

3. Luke wrote in his gospel, "_____ and _____

will pass away, but my _____ will _____ pass
away" (Luke 21:33).

God's Son does not change.

4. According to Hebrews 13:8, "Jesus Christ is the same

_____ and _____ and _____."

God remains the same.

5. In his epistle to the Hebrews, Paul emphasized God's unchange-
ableness: "In the beginning, O LORD, you laid the foundations

of the _____, and the _____ are the work of

your _____. They will _____, but you

_____; they will all _____ out like a

_____. You will roll them up like a _____; like

a _____ they will be _____. But you

_____ the _____, and your _____

will never _____" (Hebrews 1:10-12).

CHANGING SHADOWS

Below are two ideas for activities that will clearly show the changing nature of shadows.

1. Hang up a sheet. Put a light behind it. Stand between the light and the sheet. Using your hands, make shadows on the sheet. Try to shape a bird opening and closing its mouth, and a dog wiggling its ears.
2. Put a piece of paper on the ground. Push a stick through the paper and into the ground. With a pencil, draw the shadow the stick makes. Go back each hour and draw a new shadow line.

☆ APPLICATION

1. How does God differ from changing shadows?

2. How does God differ from people?

3. How can knowing that God is unchangeable help your faith grow?

4. a. What changes in your life have made you happy?

   b. What changes have made you sad?

   c. Next time you have unhappy changes, what can you remember that will help you?

CHALLENGE

Below are three synonyms for the word *unchangeable*. Using the clues given (the parts of words with their meanings), tell how these four words are related to *unchangeable*. How do they describe God?

Prefixes: *im, in, un* mean *not*
Roots: *mut* means *to change*
       alter means *to make different*
       vary means *to make changes in attributes*
Suffixes: *able* means *can* or *is able to be*

1. Immutable _____

2. Unalterable _____

3. Invariable _____

PRAYER

Dear God,
Today I just want to talk to You
about my feelings.
Friends change.
Rules change.
Plans change.
I'm disappointed. I'm confused.
Flowers die.
Pets die.
People die.
I feel lonely. I feel insecure.
Just when I'm happy something changes.
And then I'm sad.
Thank You, God, for always staying the same.
Thanks for Your love and care that never change.
Thanks for being there when I need You.
I'm happy to know I can depend on You
because You never change.
I love You, God.
Amen.

V

· · · · · · · · · · · ·

GOD IS
VICTORIOUS

He gives his king great victories.

Psalm 18:50

Rain dripped from Mindy's nose. Her hair was full of tight ringlets; her new perm smelled like rotten eggs. Red dye from her wet cheerleading skirt streaked down her legs and stained her white socks. In spite of it all, Mindy was smiling.

The score was seven to zero. As long as the guys could catch that muddy football, the girls would cheer them on.

"VICTORY! VICTORY! That's our cry. V-I-C-T-O-R-Y. Are we in it? Well, I guess. VICTORY! VICTORY! Yes! Yes! Yes!"

□　　□　　□

WHAT'S A VICTOR?

Everyone loves victory. Everyone wants to be a victor.

To discover what a victor is, unscramble these synonyms for *victor* and *victorious*. A dictionary or thesaurus will help if necessary.

1. The person who wins a contest or game is called a (N E W R I N)

   — — — — — — .

2. The team that wins a tournament is called a (P I N C H O M A)

   — — — — — — — — .

3. The army that defeats an enemy in battle is called a

   (Q E C U R R O O N) — — — — — — — — — .

4. The Christian who is victorious over temptation is

   (M I T H A R U P T N) — — — — — — — — — — .

GOD GIVES VICTORIES

In Psalm 60:12, David wrote, "With God we will gain the

_____, and he will trample down our _____."

God continually gave victories to His people. We might call these victories God's "military miracles." Let's go on a "victory hunt." Read these mini-war stories; then fill in the chart on the following page.

Victory hunt

LEADERS	ENEMIES	MIRACLES
Joshua 10:12-14		
1 Samuel 7:10-11		
1 Samuel 14:15; 14:20,23		
1 Samuel 23:4-5		
2 Samuel 5:22-25		
2 Kings 19:29, 34-35		

God gave victories in military battles. And He can give victories in other kinds of battles, too.

Victories for you

1. Paul wrote in Romans 8:37, "In all these things [trouble, hardship, persecution, famine, nakedness, danger, or sword—verse 35] we are more than _____ through him who _____ us."

2. We as believers can have confidence, because "This is the victory that has _____ the world, even our _____. Who is it that overcomes the world? Only he who _____ that Jesus is the _____ of _____" (1 John 5:4-5).

3. Because of Christ's resurrection, "_____ has been swallowed up in victory. . . . Thanks be to God! He gives us the _____ through our _____ Jesus Christ" (1 Corinthians 15:54,57).

APPLICATION

Half the fun of winning is talking about it. Have you ever been a winner in a game or contest? What was the activity? When? Where? How did you feel?

It's good to talk about success. Little successes help you develop good feelings about yourself. Victories in easy tasks help prepare you for harder contests or conflicts.

Winning a baseball game or coming in first in a spelling bee is fun, but there is another kind of battle that is more important. That's the battle against the Devil and his temptations to sin. Can you remember when you won a battle against the Devil? Over what? When? Where? How did you feel?

How to be a victor

Soldiers are outfitted for battle before they face the enemy. Christians need to put on armor to fight the Devil. Read Ephesians 6:13-18.

1. Fill in the missing letters to complete the words describing the outfit you need in order to be victorious against the Devil's schemes.
2. Write on the Devil's arrows other methods he might use to tempt you to sin.

CHALLENGE

Our sword is the Word of God. Reading the Bible and memorizing verses is the way you become equipped with your sword.

Using one of the memory methods outlined in chapters C, G, or K, memorize one of these victory verses.

"Perhaps the LORD will act in our behalf. Nothing can hinder the LORD from saving, whether by many or by few." (1 Samuel 14:6)

"With God we will gain the victory, and he will trample down our enemies." (Psalm 60:12)

"The LORD is on my side; I will not fear: what can man do unto me?" (Psalm 118:6, KJV)

"If God is for us, who can be against us?" (Romans 8:31)

PRAYER

Dear God,
You have a great record for winning battles.
I'm so glad You're on my side.
I'm so glad You promised to help me be a winner, too.
And, God, I promise to do my part.
I'll put on the outfit that will make me strong
in battles against the Devil and temptations.
In Jesus' name, amen.

W

· · · · · · · · · · · · · ·

GOD IS WISE

Oh, the depth of the riches of the
wisdom and knowledge of God!
How unsearchable his judgments,
and his paths beyond tracing out!

Romans 11:33

THE VALUE OF WISDOM

It has often been said that wisdom is the opposite of foolishness. Here's a quiz to test how wise you are. Check W for wise, or F for foolish.

W F

☐ ☐ 1. A bird builds a nest in a tree, then lays eggs on the ground.

☐ ☐ 2. A farmer plows his field, but never plants seeds.

☐ ☐ 3. A cook reads the recipe, then follows directions step by step.

☐ ☐ 4. A driver hears the seat-belt buzzer, then buckles up for the short trip across town.

☐ ☐ 5. A good swimmer reads the "No Swimming" sign and walks away, but then returns and dives in headfirst.

☐ ☐ 6. An ice skater sees the "Thin Ice" sign, then skates back toward shore.

☐ ☐ 7. An athlete trains hard for the big tournament, then stays up late the night before he plays.

☐ ☐ 8. A hiker packs his map and compass, but never looks at them when he gets lost.

☐ ☐ 9. A student takes good notes in the classroom, but doesn't study them before the exam.

☐ ☐ 10. A teenager watches a film on drunk driving, then refuses alcohol when his friends offer it to him.

Scorecard

If you selected F for 1, 2, 5, 7, 8, and 9, you are wise.
Missed one? Give yourself a B+.
Missed two? Better think twice before you act.
Missed three or more? You're skating on thin ice. Be careful.

WHAT IS WISDOM?

Wisdom is a four-pointed star. Complete the star, using the information at the left.

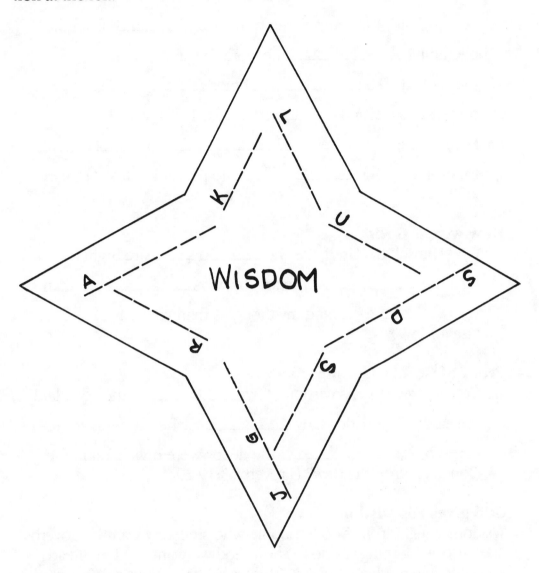

1. Knowledge—know the facts
2. Understanding—grasp the meaning of the facts
3. Sound Judgment—make sensible decisions
4. Right Action—do the right thing

Many people gain the first and second points of the wisdom star, perhaps even the third point, but lack the fourth. For example: the good swimmer read the sign, understood the meaning, made a right decision, but ultimately chose a foolish action.

Talk about the other people in the Wise-Foolish test. Why and how would you change their foolish actions?

Where does wisdom come from?

1. According to Proverbs 8:22-23, Wisdom said, "The _____ brought me forth as the _____ of his works, before his deeds of old; I was appointed from _____, from the beginning, _____ the world began."

2. Job replied, "To _____ belong _____ and power; counsel and _____ are his" (Job 12:13).

3. Daniel said, "Praise be to the _____ of _____ for ever and ever; _____ and power are his" (Daniel 2:20).

How wise is God?

4. God Himself declared, "As the _____ are higher than the _____, so are my ways _____ than your _____ and my thoughts than your _____" (Isaiah 55:9).

Proof of God's wisdom

5. Creation reveals His wisdom: "By _____ the LORD laid the earth's foundations, by _____ he set the heavens in place; by his _____ the deeps were divided, and the clouds let drop the dew" (Proverbs 3:19-20).

God gives His wisdom away

Wisdom is a gift from God to people who sincerely want it. Proverbs 2:1-6 lists eight things to do to show God we want wisdom. Read each line and meditate upon it. Think seriously about it. What does it mean? Can you say the same thing in a different way? Write down your ideas or match the phrases in the box below with each line from Proverbs 2:1-6.

How to receive wisdom

My son, if you *accept* my words and _____

_____

store up my commands within you, _____

_____

turning your ear to wisdom and _____

_____

applying your heart to understanding, and if you _____

_____

call out for insight and _____

_____

cry aloud for understanding, and if you _____

_____

look for it as for silver and _____

_____

search for it as for hidden treasure, then you will _____

_____

understand the fear of the LORD and _____

_____

find the knowledge of God. _____

_____

For the LORD *gives* wisdom, and from his mouth *come* knowledge

and understanding. _____

_____

PHRASES TO HELP YOU MEDITATE	
Ask God for wisdom.	Work hard to find it.
Pray for wisdom.	Know God's attributes and worship Him.
Discover wisdom.	All wisdom comes from God.
Seek wisdom seriously.	Wisdom is a gift from God.
Memorize Scripture.	Desire it honestly.
Believe the Bible.	Listen carefully.

CHALLENGE

King Solomon has been called the wisest man who ever lived. He wrote 3000 proverbs (wise sayings about everyday life), 1005 songs, and many scientific papers on botany and zoology.

Let's bring Solomon, his family, and friends through the *Time Tunnel* to the twentieth century so we can honor him in a special television program: "This Is Your Life, King Solomon."

The wisest man who ever lived
1 Kings 1-11 and 2 Chronicles 1-9

Chris Kelly—master of ceremonies for the program
Solomon—king of Israel; wisest man who ever lived
Bathsheba—Solomon's mother
Queen—queen of Sheba from Egypt
Hiram—king of Tyre, friend of David and Solomon
Timna—a single mother with a son (her real name is unknown)
Nathan—God's prophet to David and Solomon
Zadok—the priest, a descendant of Aaron
Narrator—storyteller

Chris: Ladies and gentlemen, our honored guest comes to us tonight from Jerusalem. Please welcome Solomon, king of Israel for forty years.

Narrator: The audience claps and cheers as Solomon comes onto the stage and sits down in the center seat.

Chris: King Solomon, tonight is your night. We want to honor you on our special television program: "This Is Your Life, King Solomon."

Solomon: I knew I was coming to the twentieth century for something special, but this certainly is a surprise.

Chris: You're not the only one from 1000 BC who is here tonight. I'm sure you'll recognize voices of family and friends as they talk about your past. First, we'll hear from a very important lady in your life.

Bathsheba: Solomon, when you were a child, you brought me happiness. When you were the king of Israel, you brought me honor and joy. I'm so proud of you.

Solomon: That could only be my mother, Bathsheba.

Narrator: Solomon stands to greet his mother as she comes from behind the stage curtain. He hugs her warmly. Then she sits down at his right side.

Chris:	Bathsheba, tell us something about your life as the wife of King David and the mother of a future king.
Bathsheba:	We were a happy family. However, the king was very busy, so I accepted the responsibility for training our four sons. God helped me bring them up to love Him and obey His laws. Solomon was a typical boy and got into his share of mischief, but he was a good student. Oh, how he loved plants and animals.
Chris:	How did your son get this title, "The Wisest Man Who Ever Lived"? Did he study under some brilliant professor or attend a famous university?
Bathsheba:	As a king's son, of course, he had the best education available. But that isn't where he gained his great wisdom.
Solomon:	My wisdom was a gift.
Chris:	A gift? Who can give wisdom as a gift?
Solomon:	God gave me wisdom.
Chris:	I don't understand.
Solomon:	One night the Lord appeared to me in a dream. He said, "Solomon, if you could ask one thing from Me, what would it be?" I was young and frightened by my new responsibilities. I asked for wisdom so I would know the difference between right and wrong.
Chris:	What did God say?
Solomon:	That dream is as clear as though I had it yesterday. God said, "Since you didn't ask to be wealthy or famous, to win wars or live a long life, I'll answer your request. I'll give you great wisdom, but I'll also fill your life with riches and honor."
Chris:	That was quite a promise. And here's someone to tell us if it came true.
Nathan:	Yes! God kept that promise. I know because I witnessed it. I was the prophet sent by God to be Solomon's spiritual guide.
Solomon:	Prophet Nathan, a man I highly respect!
Narrator:	Nathan hobbles in, leaning on his cane. Solomon stands and shakes hands with the great prophet.

Chris: Nathan, what do you remember about Solomon's wisdom?

Nathan: Daily I watched King Solomon make difficult decisions. In fact, there's one case people still talk about to this very day. Solomon, do you remember this woman?

Timna: I am grateful to you, O king. Because of you, I have a son who takes care of me in my old age.

Solomon: Oh, yes. You're one of the single mothers who came to me crying over a baby boy.

Narrator: Solomon stands as Timna walks up to him. After they shake hands, she sits beside Bathsheba.

Chris: What's this about a baby boy, Timna?

Timna: I was a poor young girl who lived in a shack with another woman. Neither of us was married, but we both were pregnant. During the same week, we gave birth to our babies. We only had one bed, so we all slept together. One morning when I awoke, the baby boy in my arms was stiff and cold. I jumped out of bed and shook him, but he wouldn't breathe. I cried as I watched the other woman nursing her baby. When I looked carefully at the dead baby, I realized he was not my son. The other woman accidentally rolled over on her baby in the night and smothered him. Then she traded our babies.

Chris: What did you do?

Timna: Neighbors arranged for us to go before the king. I sure didn't know how he could tell which baby was mine, but we went to the palace.

Solomon: After listening to the two women argue over the living baby, I ordered a soldier to bring a sword. "Divide the living child in two," I commanded, "and give half to each of these women."

Timna: I cried out, "No! No! Please don't kill the baby. Give him to the other woman."

Nathan: The other woman said, "Go ahead, divide the baby. Then neither of us shall have a son."

Timna: The king said, "Give the baby to the woman who wants him to live, for she is his mother."

Chris: That's quite a story! Solomon, I understand that your fame spread beyond the nation. Next, we're going to meet a king who visited you often.

Hiram: I watched Solomon build the Temple to his God.

Solomon: Hiram, my friend the neighboring king of Tyre. You not only watched, you were a great help.

Hiram: Solomon was wise in human relationships. He knew how to make friends. He asked me to send my woodsmen to cut cedar timber for the Temple he was going to build. He said, "No one in Israel can cut timber like you Sidonians!"

Solomon: And it was true. You cut down trees in the Lebanon mountains, floated them along the Mediterranean Sea, and delivered them to my builders.

Hiram: He was also an excellent administrator and organizer. In seven years, his work crews completed a most magnificent Temple to his God.

Chris: Solomon, stories of your wisdom and riches spread far and wide. Here's one ruler who decided to test you with some hard questions.

Queen: I heard how wonderfully the Lord had blessed Solomon with wisdom, but I couldn't believe it, so I decided to go to Jerusalem and see for myself.

Solomon: That's the beautiful and intelligent queen of Sheba.

Narrator: Solomon goes to the curtain and offers his arm to the queen. With her head erect, she glides in, the train on her robe trailing behind her. Nathan rises, giving his chair to the queen.

Queen: I remember how I traveled from Egypt with my caravan of camels bringing spices, gold, and jewels.

Solomon: And I remember how we chatted for days. I do believe you told me all your problems.

Queen: I did, and you solved every one.

Chris: What was your conclusion about Solomon's wisdom?

Queen: Only half the story had been told to me. His wisdom was far greater than any report I had ever heard.

Chris: We have one more guest. He insisted on being last.

Zadok: O king, I watched you grow from a boy to a man. I watched you worship God and I heard your words of wisdom. You were truly the wisest king who ever lived, but that's not the end of your story.

Narrator: Solomon's smile disappeared. Priest Zadok came out and stood at the end of the row.

Solomon: Yes, Priest Zadok. My life to that point was as brilliant as the north star. But you're right. My story is not finished yet.

Zadok: You gave sound advice to others, but you failed to follow it yourself. How shocked I was to see you marry an Egyptian princess! How saddened I was to see a daughter of Pharaoh sitting beside you on the throne of David!

Solomon: I was foolish to marry foreign wives and bring them into my palace.

Zadok: You had seven hundred wives and you allowed each one to worship her heathen god. That was bad enough, but your greatest sin was when you also worshiped their idols. And you did that within the sight of the Temple you had built to honor the Lord God.

Solomon: (sadly) God gave me knowledge and understanding, but I failed to make the right decisions. I failed to choose the right path.

Chris: Do you have any words of wisdom for our audience tonight?

Solomon: I'm not a good role model. I would like to tell young people: "Do what I say, but not what I do."

Chris: Well, ladies and gentlemen, our program tonight took a strange twist. We gathered to honor the wisest man of the ages only to learn that he became a fool. Priest Zadok, we'll let you have the closing words.

Zadok: I quote a proverb of King Solomon: "Trust in the LORD with all your heart and lean not on your own understanding; in all your ways acknowledge him, and he will make your paths straight."

□   □   □

Discussion

1. Why did God give wisdom to Solomon?

2. Wisdom is more than knowing what is right; it is also doing what is right. What did Solomon do that was foolish?

3. What lesson can we learn from the life of Solomon?

4. Will God give you wisdom? (See James 1:5.)

PRAYER

Praise God for His wisdom. Ask Him to give you wisdom so you will know the difference between right and wrong. Be sure to thank Him for times when He helped you make wise decisions.

X
· · · · · · · · · · · · ·
GOD IS
(E)XALTED

Be exalted, O God, above the
heavens; let your glory be over all
the earth.

Psalm 57:5

X

WHAT DOES IT MEAN TO BE EXALTED?

Perhaps a story will help us understand the word *exalted*.

Hard work brings honor

Br-ring! Br-ring! Br-ring!

A teenager groped in the darkness to turn off the alarm clock. It was a quarter of five in the morning.

Janet turned on her lamp, sat on the edge of her bed, and stretched. Dressing quickly, she grabbed her athletic bag and bounced down the stairs.

By five o'clock she was swimming laps—enough to make two miles before breakfast. After breakfast Janet was off to school. After school she was back in the pool practicing her swimming strokes for three more hours.

Dinner with the family and a couple hours of homework filled the evening. At eight o'clock she said good night.

What a tough schedule! But Janet had a goal. She wanted to win a gold medal in the 1988 Olympic Games in South Korea.

And she did.

Three times Janet Evans climbed onto the award platform. Three times the American flag floated over her head while the music of "The Star-Spangled Banner" filled the arena. Three times the officials hung a gold medal around her neck and laid a bouquet of flowers in her arms. And three times tears filled her eyes and her heart pounded as the crowd cheered. Janet waved to them triumphantly.

Standing on the highest platform, Janet Evans was declared to be a champion—the fastest female swimmer in the world. Janet was exalted by the judges, her family and friends, and the watching world.

□   □   □

Understanding words

Exalt means to praise, honor, or glorify.

- Praise—to say that a person is good or has great value; to worship in word or song.
- Honor—to show appreciation for someone for something he did with great courage or ability; to acknowledge a person's high character or position.
- Glorify—to worship through praise and honor; to show reverence and devotion.

Discussion

1. Why and how was Janet Evans exalted?

2. Which definitions above fit the story of Janet Evans?

3. Have you ever been honored? For what?

GOD IS EXALTED OVER ALL

1. After reading the Scriptures below, write what God is exalted over.

Psalm 57:5 (key verse) _____

Psalm 97:9 _____

_____

Psalm 99:2-3 _____

Why is God exalted?

2. Match these Scriptures with the correct reason as to why God is exalted. Then check whether it is related to His character or to His works.

	WHY	CHAR-ACTER	WORKS
Exodus 15:21	He is great and worthy of praise.	___	___
2 Samuel 22:47	He has done marvelous things.	___	___
Psalm 21:13	He drowned Egyptians in the Red Sea.	___	___
Psalm 48:1	He sent Jesus to earth.	___	___
Isaiah 25:1	He is our Rock and Savior.	___	___
Isaiah 33:5	He is strong and powerful.	___	___
Luke 2:20	He performs mighty miracles.	___	___
Luke 19:37	He is just and righteous.	___	___

How to exalt God

3. Psalm 95:1-2 encourages us: "Come, let us __ __ __ G __ __ __ __ __ Y to the LORD; let us shout aloud to the Rock of our salvation. Let us come before him with __ __ __ __ K __ __ __ __ V __ __ __ and __ X __ __ __ him with __ __ __ __ C and __ __ __ G ."

4. Jesus instructs us to "Let your __ __ G __ __ __ H __ __ __ before men, that they may see your __ __ O __ __ __ __ D __ and __ R __ __ __ __ __ your Father in heaven" (Matthew 5:16).

☆ APPLICATION

1. In the two verses above, how many ways can you find to praise and exalt God? What does it mean to "let your light shine"? How can that exalt God? How can your good deeds exalt God?

2. Talk about the definitions for praise, honor, and glorify on page 199. Which ones can you do when you exalt God?

3. What are your reasons for exalting God? (For example: Is it because of God's character or attributes, His creations, or what He has done for you?)

CHALLENGE

Remember the story of the ten plagues in Egypt and how God delivered His people from slavery? After that the Israelites stood on the banks of the Red Sea and watched as the waters rushed together, drowning Pharaoh and his Egyptian army. Later Moses gathered all the people together and said, "I have written a song of praise to our God. Miriam, bring your tambourine. Aaron, come and help us lead the Hebrews in this song as we worship our God."

The song of Moses
Exodus 15:1-4,6,9-13,18

Moses
Miriam
Aaron
Boys (and Men)
Girls (and Women)
All

Moses: I will sing to the LORD, for he is highly exalted.

Miriam: The horse and its rider he has hurled into the sea.

Aaron: The LORD is my strength and my song; he has become my salvation.

Moses: He is my God,

All: and I will praise him,

Moses: my father's God,

All: and I will exalt him.

Boys: The LORD is a warrior;

Girls: the LORD is his name.

X **201**

All:	I will sing to the LORD, for he is highly exalted.
Moses:	Pharaoh's chariots and his army he has hurled into the sea.
Miriam:	The best of Pharaoh's officers are drowned in the Red Sea.
Girls:	Your right hand, O LORD, was majestic in power.
Boys:	Your right hand, O LORD, shattered the enemy.
All:	I will sing to the LORD, for he is highly exalted.
Moses:	The enemy boasted, "I will pursue, I will overtake them."
Aaron:	"I will draw my sword and my hand will destroy them."
Miriam:	But you blew with your breath,
Girls:	and the sea covered them.
Boys:	They sank like lead in the mighty waters.
All:	I will sing to the LORD, for he is highly exalted.
Moses:	Who among the gods is like you, O LORD?
Miriam:	Who is like you—
Girls:	majestic in holiness,
Boys:	awesome in glory,
Girls:	working wonders?
Aaron:	You stretched out your right hand and the earth swallowed them.
Miriam:	In your unfailing love you will lead the people you have redeemed.
Moses:	In your strength you will guide them to your holy dwelling.
All:	I will sing to the LORD, for he is highly exalted.
Girls:	He is my God, and I will praise him,
Boys:	my father's God, and I will exalt him.
All:	The LORD will reign for ever and ever.

PRAYER

Our Father in Heaven,
we exalt You because You are greater
than any person, or any god, or any thing.
We want to praise You for all Your attributes
we have been studying about.
[Let family members name some they remember.]
Thank You for helping us learn
to know You better and better.
Please teach us more about who You are,
and remind us each day
of Your greatness, power, and love.
In Jesus' name, amen.

Y

GOD'S NAME IS *YAHWEH*

"This is my name forever, the name by which I am to be remembered from generation to generation."

Exodus 3:15

NAMES HAVE MEANINGS

Have you ever wondered what your name means? Baby books list hundreds of names, explain what they mean, and tell what countries they come from. Some couples use these books to help them choose names for their new babies.

Meanings of names were very important to Hebrew families. Jewish parents often gave their children names that told something about their hopes and their beliefs in God, or about the child's nature or birth. Here are some examples:

David—beloved
Daniel—God is my judge
Elizabeth—oath of God
Esau—hairy
Hannah—God has favored me
Isaac—laughter
Jesus—to save
Mary—bitterness
Samuel—God has heard

Think of Bible characters with these names. How do these names fit each person? Why do you think parents chose the name?

DO GODS HAVE NAMES?

In every land and in every century, people have worshiped many gods. And each god has a name. Draw a line to match the names of these gods with the right description.

GODS	DESCRIPTION
Allah	Egyptian sun god
Baal	Roman god of love
Brahman	Muslim god
Buddha	Greek god of sleep
Cupid	Phoenician god that Jezebel worshiped
Hypnos	Roman god of war
Mars	Greek ruler of all gods
Ra	an oriental god
Zeus	Hindu god

DOES OUR GOD HAVE A PERSONAL NAME?

Christians worship *God Almighty* and capitalize the word *God* to show He is different from pagan gods. But, does God have another name? Use the *King James Version* for these answers.

1. Exodus 3:14 says, "And God said unto Moses,

   _____."

2. God said to Moses, "And I appeared unto Abraham, unto Isaac,

   and unto Jacob, by the _____ of _____

   _____; but by my name _____ was I not

   known to them" (Exodus 6:3).

3. The psalmist wrote Psalm 83:18, "That men may know that thou,

   whose _____ alone is _____, art the

   _____ _____ over all the earth."

4. Isaiah declared in a song of praise, "Behold, God is my salvation;

   I will trust, and not be afraid: for the LORD _____ is my
   strength and my song; he also is become my salvation" (Isaiah
   12:2).

5. We are instructed to "Trust ye in the _____ for ever: for

   in the LORD _____ is everlasting strength" (Isaiah 26:4).

What does Jehovah mean?

Jehovah is the personal name of the true Creator God. It is the name by which God made Himself known.

In Exodus 3:14, God said, "I AM WHO I AM." God is dependent upon nobody, upon nothing except Himself and His own will.

Jehovah means "I AM"—"I am always present." God is one who exists now, who always has existed, and who will never cease to exist. Jehovah is here. Jehovah is eternal.

Jehovah means "I AM"—"I am actively present." God is always deeply involved in the lives of His people. He cares for them and loves them, and promises to protect them. Jehovah is unchangeable. His promises are true.

Where did the name "Jehovah" come from?

The Hebrew alphabet has twenty-six characters standing for twenty-six consonants. What about the vowels? Hebrew vowels are dots placed above or below consonant characters. When God said "I AM," Moses wrote down the Hebrew characters for YHWH:

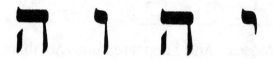

Because no dots were included, there were no vowels.

The Jews didn't want to pronounce God's name because they believed it was too holy to be spoken. They were afraid of breaking the Third Commandment, which said, "You shall not misuse the name of the LORD your God, for the LORD will not hold anyone guiltless who misuses his name" (Exodus 20:7).

How did they read the Scriptures?

Another Hebrew word *Adonai* meant "Lord." To help people read the Scriptures aloud, the vowel dots from *Adonai* were placed above the letters *YHWH.* This showed readers they should say the word *Adonai. YHWH* was never intended to be pronounced with these vowels from *Adonai.*

But something strange happened. Years later, English translators put those vowels between the letters *YHWH* and formed the name *Yahweh* (YAW way). Some translators spelled it Jehovah.

So *Yahweh* or *Jehovah* is God's holy name. It's the name by which God made Himself known and by which He wants to be remembered forever.

Names used by today's translations

Many translations use LORD for the Hebrew letters *YHWH.*

Fill in the blanks below, and remember to write *Yahweh* in place of *the LORD.*

1. Hosea 12:5 says, "The LORD God Almighty, _____ is his

   _____ of renown!"

2. Joshua said to the people, "Now fear _____ and serve

   him with all _____. Throw away the _____
   your forefathers worshiped beyond the River and in Egypt, and

   serve _____" (Joshua 24:14).

Discussion

3. What do you understand about God's personal name?

4. The meaning of a name often reveals the nature or character of a person. Does God's name *Yahweh* remind you of any of God's attributes you have studied?

☆APPLICATION

1. Read or quote the Third Commandment (Exodus 20:7).

2. How do people break that commandment today?

3. When and how can you use God's name so that it pleases Him?

PRAYER

O God, whose name is holy,
and its meaning so very special,
You are greater than all creation.
You do not need anybody or anything to exist,
for You have always lived and You will never die.
I'm so glad You are alive today
and that You care about everything I do.
Come live in my heart
and be a part of my daily activities.
Help me to speak Your name with respect and love,
remembering that You are my Creator and my Lord.
In Jesus' name, amen.

Z

GOD IS ZEALOUS

The zeal of the LORD Almighty will accomplish this.

2 Kings 19:31

Z

GOD IS EAGER TO SAVE

Zeal and *zealous*—Do you know what they mean? Here's a story that will explain them better than a hundred definitions. It's a story about a coonhound. Let's call him:

Zealous Zeke

"That raccoon got into my hen house again last night. He ate the eggs and killed another chicken," said Nellie.

"And he's ruining my cornfield," said her husband, Joe. "I guess it's time for a coon hunt."

After dark, Joe took his rifle out of its hiding place and placed some ammunition into his pocket.

"Come on, Zeke," Joe called to his dog. "Let's go find the coon that's vandalizing our farm."

Zeke bounded to Joe's side, his long ears flopping and his tail wagging with enthusiasm. Zeke knew the rifle meant a night of running and hunting.

The autumn moon was full and bright. Joe and Zeke walked through the cornfield. When Zeke picked up the smell of the coon, he raced for the nearby woods.

Joe followed awhile, then he sat down and leaned against a huge tree trunk while Zeke searched the woods.

All night Zeke sniffed the ground for the coon tracks. Sometimes he'd sniff the air. The determined hound ran for miles, circling through the woods. Puffing and panting, he returned to his master.

But Zeke wouldn't rest. He was relentless in his search for the coon. That was his job. He was eager and anxious to find the coon.

Down by the stream, the scent became stronger. He followed the fresh tracks until he came to a big oak tree where the scent stopped. He knew the coon was up that tree. Zeke sat near the trunk of the tree, lifted his nose to the sky, and let out a long, deep howl. He kept baying until Joe arrived.

In the bright moonlight, Joe could see the coon sitting on a branch. One shot brought it down. He picked up the coon and dropped it into a sack.

"You're a persistent and hard-working hound," Joe said as he patted Zeke on the head. "You never give up the chase until you tree a coon."

◻ ◻ ◻

Discussion

1. What was Zeke's goal?

2. Why did he reach his goal?

3. Have you ever been zealous about something? What was it? What did you do that indicated you were zealous?

QUALITIES OF ZEALOUSNESS

1. Unscramble words from the story that describe Zealous Zeke.

a. A G E R E

—— —— —— —— ——

b. X A I S U N O

—— —— —— —— —— —— ——

c. T R E S P I N T E S

—— —— —— —— —— —— —— —— —— ——

d. S L E N R S L E T E

—— —— —— —— —— —— —— —— —— ——

e. M E D I T N E D E R

—— —— —— —— —— —— —— —— ——

f. T H E N U S T I A S C I

—— —— —— —— —— —— —— —— —— —— —— —— ——

God is zealous about His people.

2. Does God have a *goal?*
   In Isaiah 46:4, God says, "I have made you and I will

   _____ you; I will _____ you and I will

   _____ you."

Z²¹³

3. Does God *feel strongly* about His goal?

God speaks concerning His people: "I _____ make an

_____ covenant with them: I will _____ stop

doing _____ to them" (Jeremiah 32:40).

4. Is God *anxious* and *determined* to reach His goal?

The Apostle Peter writes, "He is _____ with you, not

wanting anyone to _____, but _____ to come
to repentance" (2 Peter 3:9).

God is zealous as a Protector.

5. God promised to save His people by being their warrior.
   a. According to Isaiah 59:17, "He put on righteousness as his

   _____, and the _____ of salvation on his

   head; he put on the _____ of vengeance and

   wrapped himself in _____ as in a _____."

   b. We read in 2 Kings 19:31,35, "The _____ of the LORD

   _____ will accomplish this. . . . That night the angel

   of the _____ went out and put to death a

   _____ and _____

   _____ men in the _____ camp."

God is zealous as a Savior.

6. God promised to save the people from their sins.
   a. Concerning the birth of Christ, Isaiah 9:6-7 states, "For to us a

   _____ is born, to us a son is given, and the government will be on his shoulders. And he will be called

   _____ _____, _____

   _____, _____ _____,

   _____ of _____. . . . The _____ of

   the LORD _____ will accomplish this."

b. An angel of the Lord told Joseph, "She will give birth to a son, and you are to give him the name _____, because he will _____ his people from their _____" (Matthew 1:21).

c. The Lord says in Revelation 3:20, "Here I am! I _____ at the door and _____. If anyone hears my _____ and opens the door, I will _____ and _____ with him, and he with me."

God is zealous as a Rewarder.
Most awards are given to people who do something very difficult. But God is so zealous to bless His people, He rewards us for small tasks that we do.

7. One example is in Matthew 10:42. God will reward us if we

_____ .

☆ APPLICATION

1. Revelation 3:20 paints a picture that shows the zealousness of God through His Son, Jesus.
   a. Talk about the symbols. What is the door? What is Jesus actually doing? Where will He go? How can He get in? What does it mean to "eat with Him"?

   b. Where can you see the qualities of zealousness in this picture? Is there a goal? Patience? Persistence? Eagerness? Determination to reach His goal?

2. God is still zealous about *saving* people from sin, *protecting* His people, and *rewarding* those who serve Him.
   a. Can you think of any experience in your life that might show God's zealousness?

   b. If not, determine as a family to watch for evidence of God's zealousness in the future, and then talk about it together.

PRAYER

Dear God,
I didn't know You were so zealous.
I knew You loved all the people You created,
but I didn't realize just how hard You work to save us.
Or how determined You are to protect us from evil.
Or how eager You are to send Your blessings
when our deeds for You are so simple and small.
I'm thankful for Your zealousness, Lord.
My heart is full of love for You.
I appreciate You. Thank You, God, for showing
Your wonderful attributes to me.
Help me to remember them,
and to honor You in all I do.
In Jesus' name, amen.

• • • Summary of God's Attributes • • •

Psalm 145 is a praise song of David. It is full of the attributes of God. You'll find at least one attribute in every verse. Some are repeated several times. You'll even find some attributes you didn't study in this book.

As you read the psalm, fill in the blanks with the attributes that come to your mind. Not every family member will think of the same attributes. See how many different ones you can find.

Psalm 145

1. I will exalt you, my God the King; I will praise your name for ever and ever. _____

2. Every day I will praise you and extol your name for ever and ever. _____

3. Great is the LORD and most worthy of praise; his greatness no one can fathom. _____

4. One generation will commend your works to another; they will tell of your mighty acts. _____

5. They will speak of the glorious splendor of your majesty, and I will meditate on your wonderful works. _____

6. They will tell of the power of your awesome works, and I will proclaim your great deeds. _____

7. They will celebrate your abundant goodness and _____

   joyfully sing of your righteousness. _____

8. The LORD is gracious and compassionate, _____

   slow to anger and rich in love. _____

9. The LORD is good to all; _____

   he has compassion on all he has made. _____

10. All you have made will praise you, O Lord; your saints will extol you.

_____

11. They will tell of the glory of your kingdom and

_____

speak of your might,

_____

12. so that all men may know of your mighty acts and the

_____

glorious splendor of your kingdom.

_____

13. Your kingdom is an everlasting kingdom,

_____

and your dominion endures through all generations.

_____

The Lord is faithful to all his promises

_____

and loving toward all he has made.

_____

14. The Lord upholds all those who fall and lifts up all who are bowed down.

_____

15. The eyes of all look to you, and you give them their food at the proper time.

_____

16. You open your hand and satisfy the desires of every living thing.

_____

17. The Lord is righteous in all his ways

_____

and loving toward all he has made.

_____

18. The Lord is near to all who call on him,

_____

to all who call on him in truth.

_____

19. He fulfills the desires of those who fear him;

_____

he hears their cry and saves them.

_____

20. The Lord watches over all who love him,

_____

but all the wicked he will destroy.

_____

21. My mouth will speak in praise of the Lord. Let every creature praise his holy name for ever and ever.

_____

CLOSING PRAYER AND PRAISE

Assign the verses of Psalm 145 to different family members. Then read it as a choral reading.

Chapter A, page 20: What's the secret message?

1. Pharaoh's heart
2. East wind
3. Gods of Egypt
4. Chariot wheels
5. Jordan River
6. Enemies
7. Nations
8. Boy lying dead
9. Leprosy
10. Every creature
11. Violent storm

Power and might are in your hand, and no one can withstand you. (2 Chronicles 20:6)

Chapter B, page 30: Counting Abraham's blessings

BOY
LAND
SERVANTS
SILVER
SHEEP
LIVESTOCK
NATIONS
KINGS
OFFSPRING

Chapter D, page 47: Geometric code

If God delivered Daniel from the lions, Peter from prison, and Hebrews from slavery, I know God can help me when I am in trouble.

Chapter E, page 54: God is eternal.

CODE

1. G	5. S	9. R	13. O
2. T	6. H	10. L	14. D
3. E	7. A	11. B	15. V
4. Y	8. N	12. F	16. I

Chapter F, page 59: Characteristics of our heavenly Father

Characteristics of our heavenly Father

5. After reading each Scripture, draw a line to the matching trait.

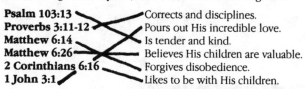

Psalm 103:13 — Corrects and disciplines.
Proverbs 3:11-12 — Pours out His incredible love.
Matthew 6:14 — Is tender and kind.
Matthew 6:26 — Believes His children are valuable.
2 Corinthians 6:16 — Forgives disobedience.
1 John 3:1 — Likes to be with His children.

Chapter F, page 62: Famous Bible families

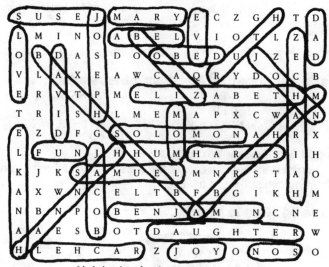

(dad, daughter, fun, home, joy, love, mom, son)

Chapter G, pages 65-66: Discovering that God is gracious

a. See trouble and grief; Helper of the fatherless
b. Showed concern
c. A forgiving God; Slow to anger; Abounding in love; Did not desert them
d. Provides food; Remembers His covenant

Chapter G, page 67: Word picture of a gracious God

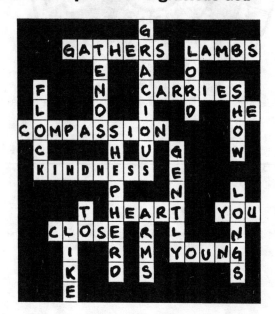

Chapter I, page 81: What makes idols different from God?

1. a. Hands, men, speak, see, hear
   b. Move, answer, save, troubles

Chapter I, pages 81-82: What makes the Lord God different from other gods?

2. a. Rescued, people
   b. Deeds, works
   c. Holy
   d. Keeps, love
   e. Savior

Chapter J, page 90: God deals righteously.

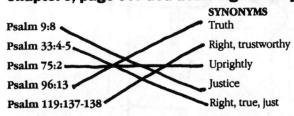

SYNONYMS

Psalm 9:8 — Truth
Psalm 33:4-5 — Right, trustworthy
Psalm 75:2 — Uprightly
Psalm 96:13 — Justice
Psalm 119:137-138 — Right, true, just

Chapter J, page 91: Tic-tac-toe code

God's justice is as high as the heavens, as deep as the ocean, and as solid as the mountains. (From Psalm 71:9 and 36:6.)

Chapter K, page 94: Famous kings

1. Cole   3. Arthur   5. Henry   7. Ahab
2. Midas   4. Saul   6. Herod   8. David

Chapter K, page 94: God is King over all.

DESCRIPTION

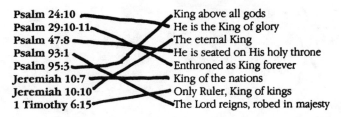

Psalm 24:10 — King above all gods
Psalm 29:10-11 — He is the King of glory
Psalm 47:8 — The eternal King
Psalm 93:1 — He is seated on His holy throne
Psalm 95:3 — Enthroned as King forever
Jeremiah 10:7 — King of the nations
Jeremiah 10:10 — Only Ruler, King of kings
1 Timothy 6:15 — The Lord reigns, robed in majesty

Chapter K, page 97: Hidden royalty words

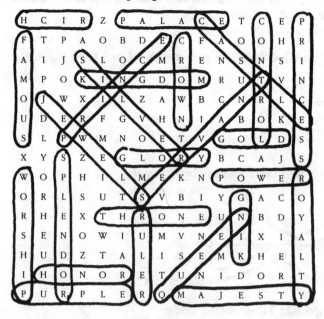

Chapter L, page 101: Defining the love of God

	QUOTATION	DEFINITION
Psalm 103:8	"unfailing love . . . will not be shaken"	continues on forever
Psalm 103:11	"his love endures forever"	unchanging; always the same
Psalm 106:1	"high as the heavens are above the earth"	overflowing
Isaiah 54:10	"demonstrates his own love. . . . While we were still sinners"	never stopping; unceasing
Jeremiah 31:3	"abounding in love"	cannot be earned; unconditional
Romans 5:8	"I have loved you with an everlasting love"	too great to be measured

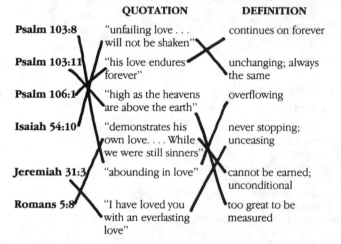

Chapter L, page 102: A word picture of a loving God

Chapter N, page 117: Where are You, God?

a. with
b. among
c. wherever
d. right hand
e. close
f. near
g. not far
h. nearby, far away, Heaven, earth
Grand answer: God is everywhere.

Chapter N, page 119: God is near. (rebus)

1. Abednego
2. Daniel
3. Meshach
4. Belteshazzar
5. Hebrews
6. Spirit

Chapter O, page 123: Omniscient acrostic

THOUGHTS
MOTIVE
MIND
SIN
WAYS
SECRETS
MYSTERIES
HEART
MANKIND
STEP

Chapter O, page 124: Runaways

Chapter P, pages 128-130: How God supplied needs

1. a. They would become slaves.
2. e. Elisha
3. j. Kerith
4. h. ravens
5. h. Jericho
6. v. salt
7. o. God
Hebrew name for God: Jehovah

Chapter Q, page 142: Message from Jesus

1. hour
2. poor
3. earth
4. found
5. poetry
6. yesterday
7. gracious
8. donkey
9. woman
10. root
11. holy

When you pray, go into your room, close the door, and pray to your Father (Matthew 6:6).

Chapter R, page 147: A Refuge for people

1. Shield: Psalm 119:114
2. Fortress: Jeremiah 16:19
3. Eagle's wings: Psalm 91:4
4. Everlasting arms: Deuteronomy 33:27
5. Shade: Isaiah 25:4
6. Strong tower: Proverbs 18:10
7. Stronghold: Psalm 9:9
8. Rock: Psalm 71:3

Chapter R, page 149: A message in Morse code

God is my refuge. This I know.
He will be with me, wherever I go.

Chapter T, page 163: Synonyms for faithfulness

Deuteronomy 7:9	WHO SAID IT?	SYNONYMS FOR FAITHFUL
Deuteronomy 7:9	*Levites*	Not one word has failed
Joshua 21:45	*Paul*	Every promise was fulfilled
2 Samuel 7:28	*Moses*	He will do it
1 Kings 8:56	*Jesus*	Keeps His covenant of love
Nehemiah 9:8	*Joshua*	Kept Your promise
John 8:26	*Solomon*	Trustworthy
1 Thessalonians 5:24	*David*	Reliable

Chapter T, page 169: A maze of choices

Chapter U, page 172: Things that change form

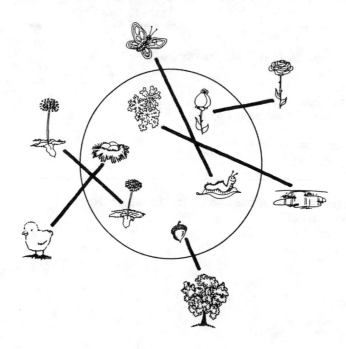

Chapter U, page 173: Things that change shape or size

1. cloud
2. volcano
3. dune
4. forest
5. river
6. cow (bull, seal, whale), deer; animals
7. man, woman; people

Chapter U, pages 174-175: Pictures of change (rebus)

Earth, top, sun; earth, sun, set; sky, shadows; trees, rocks, houses, people; sun, east, west, shadows; shadows, minute; shadows, Indians, time; sundial, angle, shadows, sun; angle, sun, sky; shadows; man.

Chapter V, page 180: What's a victor?

1. Winner
2. Champion
3. Conqueror
4. Triumphant

Chapter V, page 182: How to be a victor

Helmet of *salvation*
Prayer
Shield of *faith*
Breastplate of *righteousness*
Belt of *truth*
Sword of the Spirit is the *Word.*
Shoes are the gospel of *peace.*

Chapter V, page 182: How to be a victor

Helmet of *salvation*
Prayer
Shield of *faith*
Breastplate of *righteousness*
Belt of *truth*
Sword of the Spirit is the *Word.*
Shoes are the gospel of *peace.*

Chapter W, page 187: What is wisdom? (star)

Chapter W, page 189: How to receive wisdom
(possible order of suggested answers)

Believe the Bible.
Memorize Scripture.
Listen carefully.
Desire it honestly.
Ask God for wisdom.
Pray for wisdom.
Seek wisdom seriously.
Work hard to find it.
Know God's attributes and worship Him.
Discover wisdom.
Wisdom is a gift from God.
All wisdom comes from God.

Chapter X, page 200: Why is God exalted?

	WHY	CHAR-ACTER	WORKS
Exodus 15:21	He is great and worthy of praise.	X	—
2 Samuel 22:47	He has done marvelous things.	—	X
Psalm 21:13	He drowned Egyptians in the Red Sea.	—	X
Psalm 48:1	He sent Jesus to earth.	—	X
Isaiah 25:1	He is our Rock and Savior.	X	—
Isaiah 33:5	He is strong and powerful.	X	—
Luke 2:20	He performs mighty miracles.	—	X
Luke 19:37	He is just and righteous.	X	—

Chapter Y, page 206: Do gods have names?

GODS	DESCRIPTION
Allah	Egyptian sun god
Baal	Roman god of love
Brahman	Muslim god
Buddha	Greek god of sleep
Cupid	Phoenician god that Jezebel worshiped
Hypnos	Roman god of war
Mars	Greek ruler of all gods
Ra	an oriental god
Zeus	Hindu god

Chapter Z, page 213: Qualities of zealousness

a. Eager
b. Anxious
c. Persistent
d. Relentless
e. Determined
f. Enthusiastic

Summary, pages 217-218: Psalm 145 (possible answers)

1. King
2. Exalted
3. Great (Wise)
4. Almighty
5. Majestic
   Miracle-worker
6. Omnipotent (Almighty
7. Good
   Righteous (Holy)
8. Gracious (Kind)
   Compassionate
   Patient
   Loving
9. Good (Just and fair)
   Compassionate (Kind)
10. Exalted
11. King
    Omnipotent (Almighty)
12. Omnipotent
    King
13. Everlasting
    Eternal
    Faithful (True)
    Loving Creator
14. Helper (Deliverer)
15. Provider
16. Blessing-giver
17. Righteous (Holy)
    Creator
18. Omnipresent (Near)
19. Provider
    Savior (Deliverer)
20. Protector
    Just Judge
21. Holy